If My
Parents Knew . . .

Other resources from Rodney Gage

Books and Booklets:
Let's Talk about AIDS and Sex
Meeting Your Child's Unspoken Needs
How to Be Born Again
Go Tell Student Manual

Videos:
Let's Talk About AIDS and Sex
Wise Up School Assembly (Teenagers and Drinking)

Audio Cassette Album:
How to Keep Your Kids Off Alcohol and Drugs

To schedule Rodney to come to your church or school campus, to order any of these materials, or to receive a free copy of *Straight Talk Newsletter for Parents*, write or call:

The Rodney Gage Association
P. O. Box 820553
Fort Worth, TX 76182
1-800-880-0254

IF MY PARENTS KNEW...

Discovering Your Teenager's Unspoken Needs

Rodney Gage

THOMAS NELSON PUBLISHERS

Nashville • Atlanta • London • Vancouver

Published in Nashville, Tennessee, by Thomas Nelson, Inc., Publishers, and distributed in Canada by Word Communications, Ltd., Richmond, British Columbia, and in the United Kingdom by Word (UK), Ltd., Milton Keynes, England.

Scripture quotations are from the NEW KING JAMES VERSION of the Bible. Copyright © 1979, 1980, 1982, 1990, Thomas Nelson, Inc., Publishers.

Library of Congress Cataloging-in-Publication Data

Gage, Rodney R. 1965-
    If my parents knew— : discovering your teenager's unspoken needs / Rodney R. Gage.
        p. cm.
    Includes bibliographical references.
    ISBN 0—7852-7825-7 (pb.)
    1. Teenagers. 2. Communication. 3. Parent and teenager. I. Title.
HQ799.15.G34   1995
306.874—dc20   95-3930
                                                                    CIP

Printed in the United States of America
2 3 4 5 6 7 - 01 00 99 98 97 96

This book is dedicated to my parents, Dr. Freddie and Barbara Gage. There is not enough paper to share how I really feel about my parents. I am so grateful for the investment they have made in my life. They have seen the fruit of their lives and their prayers, as all four of their sons are in the ministry sharing the gospel of Christ.

You have been my greatest inspiration. I love you with all my heart!

Contents

Acknowledgments

As you will see, the pages of this book have been shaped by thousands of young people who talked to me about their hopes and heartaches, their dreams and dreads. I am very grateful for their honesty and insights.

I have also had the privilege of talking with many parents who genuinely want to communicate love and acceptance to their teenage children. Their hopes for their children are an inspiration to me.

Several good friends have taken the time to write their stories for this book. They have shared the confusion and heartache of their misguided decisions, and they have also communicated the life-changing power of God's grace. I am indebted to these dear and vulnerable friends. In compiling the letters from young people and their parents, many youth pastors and teachers have helped me.

I particularly want to thank Pat Springle of Baxter Press for his time and energy in helping me complete this manuscript. My wife, Michelle, has been the greatest encourager in the world to me. She supports my ministry as I travel across the country speaking to thousands of young people.

More than anything, I want to thank Jesus for giving me the opportunity to write this book. I pray God will use it to give hope and encouragement to everyone who reads its pages!

Introduction

Have you told your parents what you're telling me?" I've asked hundreds of young people who pour out their hearts to me. Most of them silently shake their heads.

"No," they then mutter. "No, I haven't."

I can't tell you how many times I have walked away from a conversation with a teenager wishing I could tape-record it and send it to the parents—to you! I have to be honest with you: As I have talked to thousands of young people and parents, I have felt tremendously frustrated by the hurt and confusion caused by their lack of communication.

Out of this frustration—and the hope it has produced in me—I have written this book. I didn't want to write just another book about parenting teenagers. I wanted you to hear from the teenagers themselves: their hopes, their hurts, their dreams, and their disappointments.

As you read these pages, you will see many letters and poems. I have asked young people at summer camps, in church youth groups, and in classrooms to communicate with me. Most wrote letters to me, some sent me letters they wrote to their parents, and some wrote poetry to express their feelings about their parents.

Also, I asked some parents to write me about their teenagers, and I interviewed some parents and their teenagers to get both sides of a particularly poignant story.

The names and places mentioned in these letters and stories have been changed to protect anonymity, and I have edited some of them for length. You will see, however, that I left the grammar and spelling as the teenagers wrote them so you can read these wonderful letters essentially as I have them stacked here on my desk.

In these pages, teenagers speak to you from their hearts, in their own words, and from their own perspective of life. They graphically express their anger and hurt, their hopes and dreams. I have made no attempt to question their truthfulness. Some may have colored the facts to make themselves appear innocent and good, but my experience with these young people tells me that these letters and stories represent an accurate picture of the way they really think and feel.

Some of these letters will make you laugh. Some will warm your heart with their genuine love and kindness. But some will break your heart as you read of the loneliness, confusion, and heartache they feel. My goal is not to make you feel guilty or communicate that you need to be "the perfect parent." My reason for writing this book is to help open lines of communication and understanding between parents and their teenagers.

Parents don't have to be perfect to have a rich, meaningful relationship with their teenagers. They only need to have the courage to listen, speak the truth, and discover the unspoken needs in their kids' lives. God is still in the business of changing lives. The beautiful thing about families is that He can work through an individual—like you—to help others in the family experience His love, strength, and hope.

Questions and exercises are included at the end of each chapter to encourage you to apply the principles found in the book. Some people use these for individual reflection, and some couples use them to stimulate interaction and planning. In addition, I encourage you to use this book for small group discussion. You may want to have several couples gather to discuss selected chapter assignments each week, or your church may choose to use this material in a Sunday school class for parents of teenagers. Whether you reflect on these questions and exercises alone or with others, they will stimulate your thinking, facilitate your application, and encourage your heart.

PART 1

They Need Us to Understand!

CHAPTER 1

Stop, Look, and Listen!

Do you know what I am?" a teenager once asked. "I'm a comma."

"What do you mean?" the listener replied.

"Well, whenever I talk to my dad, he stops talking and makes a 'comma.' But when I'm finished, he starts right up again as if I hadn't said a thing. I'm just a comma in the middle of his speeches."[1]

I believe the saddest words in the English language are *if only*. In the past few years, I have had the privilege of speaking to over two million students across America, and I have thought on countless occasions, *If parents only knew what their kids are telling me!*

You might be thinking, *What can Rodney Gage tell me about my own child that I don't already know?* But many parents—I would say *most* parents—don't really know their teenagers' unspoken thoughts, feelings, and desires. In conversation after conversation after I speak to school assemblies and churches, young people say to me:

"I can't talk to my parents."

"My parents don't have time for me."

"My parents don't understand me."

"My parents just don't care."

Many parents who read these statements respond, "Those kids don't really mean what they are saying, do they?" Unfortunately, I believe they do. Most teenagers feel misunderstood and disconnected. The fact that you are reading this book means this last statement isn't true of you, but you may learn a lot from reading the stories in this book about how teenagers—even yours—think and feel.

Teenagers genuinely want to be understood. This letter expresses the sadness and confusion of not being able to talk to a father.

Dear Rodney,

My parents are great. They listen, and understand when I need them, and they are always there for me. At least my mom is. My dad is a great guy, and I know he loves me because he tells me all the time. He just doesn't seem to want to listen to me, or be there when I have a problem. He listens to the words I say, but he doesn't always listen to how I feel. Don't get me wrong. I love my Dad. We just can't relate to each other anymore. I want to talk to him about how I feel, but I just don't know how to get him to listen.

Please help me. I don't know what to do. I've prayed about it, but I've never been too good at hearing God's response. I know if I pray enough and listen hard enough sooner or later I will hear God speak to me, and I'll be able to relate better to my dad.

Sincerely,
Tracy

When parents are too busy to listen, kids assume there's something wrong with themselves. This letter expresses that self-blame for the absence of communication with parents.

Dear Rodney,

I wish sometimes I would have the time or the desire to talk with my parents about my future. There are times when I feel I have expressed my feelings and they have gone unnoticed. I feel dumb telling them again. I'm afraid of being a pest. I love my parents very much and it is hard to find something "wrong" with them, but they just don't seem to listen to me when I want to tell them how I really feel about things.

Lynda

Teenagers feel pulled in two directions. No, that's too mild. They feel like the rope in a tractor pull! They want to go in both directions, but they feel like they are being ripped apart. They still want to be connected to their parents, especially in early adolescence, but at the same time they are getting their feet wet in their quest for independence.

Later, they aren't so timid. They dive in. The internal drive to pull away and establish a separate identity causes them to question their parents' values and behaviors. Communication is often a casualty of this tumultuous time. Adolescents want to feel loved and accepted by their parents, but they also demand their freedom. Often, parents feel confused, angry, and alone. Most parents genuinely want to communicate with their teenagers, but they don't know how. In fact, their attempts at communication are often counterproductive, and they drive their kids farther away.

Sometimes parents think their kids don't notice very much. One father told me, "James lives in his own world. He doesn't even know if I'm alive or dead most of the time."

But James told me a very different story. He talked about how much he wants to be a part of his dad's life, but that his dad seems too preoccupied with work. The message they sent each other was: "Stay out of my life. I don't care about you!" But what they really felt was: "I really love you and need you. I want a rich and real relationship with you!"

Some of the distance in teen-parent communication is natural, normal, and healthy. It is a vital part of the young person's process of maturity and independence. But much of this communication gap is the by-product of hurt, misunderstanding, and unhealthy reactions intended to keep from being hurt again. We desperately need to learn the difference between the two. In many ways, that's what this book is all about.

Part of the communication problem is the spiraling effect of misperceptions. Parents and young people want to be loved and accepted, but they react by withdrawing or attacking when they don't feel that love. These responses fuel more reactions and the process continues to escalate until they must ask themselves, "What in the world is wrong with us? How did we get in such a mess?"

Some parents are caught up in their own lives. They are self-focused because of heartaches they've experienced. Perhaps they've been through a painful divorce, or they feel stuck in a difficult marriage, or another child is having problems, or they feel pressure at work. Perhaps they are trying to find their own identity through achievements at work or in other relationships. Or perhaps they have withdrawn into a cocoon of isolation and hopelessness, watching television to pass the time and dull the pain. Some parents may feel so hopeless that they don't even care about their children anymore, but the vast majority genuinely care. They are just too overwhelmed to know how to show it.

The other side of the equation is that adolescents need to become more self-sufficient and independent during this period of their lives. Questioning authority—especially parental authority—is a normal part of their growing independence. The perception that "My parents don't care," or "They don't understand," helps young people break away because it is easier to become independent if they believe their parents are insensitive or stupid. These perceptions, then, can be a normal part of an adolescent's questioning of authority and can legitimize the behavior of pulling away.

A friend of mine told me that his twelve-year-old son suddenly expressed dislike for his favorite teams. For years, the father and son had rooted for the same teams, but early adolescence drove the child to rebel against his dad's teams. That's a very little thing, but in sports-minded families, small wars develop over team loyalty!

Similarly, parents need to be very careful about telling their teenage kids they can't listen to certain music or hang around certain people. The dynamic of independence sometimes turns the forbidden into the desirable.

Tension often centers on the parents' desire for control. When their compliant, cheerful children suddenly become defiant "monsters," tempers snap. Parents turn up the control. The kids feel attacked and rebel even more. At this point, parental requests for communication are often met with angry outbursts, sullen quiet, or sarcasm. So the parents turn up the heat again.

I have had thousands of parents come to me and, with tears in their eyes, tell me how they would give anything to communicate with their kids. This book is for you. But I don't want you to hear from me only. I want you to hear from the mouths, pens, and hearts of young people who are just as desperate to communicate with you as you may be to communicate with them. However, we need to start with this basic understanding: The normal, healthy nature of adolescence is to become more independent. Parents must understand—and accept—that fact if real communication is to become a reality.

The environment of the home is the critical factor in determining the direction of a young person's life. Other factors may contribute, but the strength, perception, and skills acquired in the home are most important. Author and motivational speaker, Zig Ziglar, quotes an anonymous writer:

In every home there are two microphones per child—one in each ear. These highly sensitive instruments pick up the table prayers, the songs sung, ordinary conversation, and all types of language. These all-hearing microphones transmit all they hear to highly impressionable minds. These sounds then become the vocabulary of the child and his basis for action.[2]

In his milestone book, *The First Three Years of Life*, Dr. Burton White states that a child's sense of stability and self-image are established in the first three years. Commenting on this crucial period of development, Zig Ziglar adds a year to Dr. White's observation and writes, "The education a child receives from his parents the first four years of life is more significant than four years of college."[3] Dr. Joyce Brothers has observed the fact that a person's self-concept shapes virtually every behavior and belief. She wrote, "The profession you choose, the habits you acquire, the way you dress, your moral conduct, and the person you marry will be determined by the image you have of yourself."[4]

In fact, some of the problems we see in our adolescent children are the consequences of deficiencies in these early years. This observation isn't meant to lay a guilt trip on anyone! It is only meant to show how important modeling is for our children.

If you find yourself needing to make amends for the past, now is the time to do it. Just as the Lord's mercies are new every morning, each of us has the opportunity to begin again every day. And no matter how badly we have modeled love, acceptance, and strength in the past, today we can begin to learn to treat our children with respect and love. Overcoming the past is difficult, but thousands of mended relationships testify that it is possible. And worth it.

In this book, we will hear from young people how they think and feel about life. Some of their letters are quite positive and hopeful. Some reveal desperation, or worse, hopelessness. The messages of these letters are not always reflected in the outward appearance of the teenager. Sometimes, the most hopeless heart is wrapped in an exterior of smiles, scholastic achievement, athletic performance, and social skills. In this sense, the old saying is true: Don't judge a book by its cover!

Reflection/Discussion Questions

1. As you begin this book, what are some things you hope to learn?
2. What are some changes you would like to make in your relationship with your teenager?
3. Has your teenager ever said something like, "You just don't understand!"? If so, how did you feel? How did you respond?
4. Who is the person who has been most understanding and kind to you? What did this person do to make you feel accepted and loved? How can you practice some of these qualities in your relationship with your teenager?

CHAPTER 2

What If They Really Did Tell You?!

Teenagers are a puzzle—to themselves, their friends, and their parents! They are going through cataclysmic changes, and they often don't understand their own thoughts and feelings. The vast majority of parents genuinely want to communicate with these strange and wonderful (sometimes more one than the other) creatures, but understanding can be elusive.

An eighth-grade girl wrote this poem about the powerful and conflicting emotions she feels.

A Different View of My Life

My life has been a maze of truth,
A story yet untold.
They always see the outside part,
The girl who laughs and smiles throughout the day.
It's deep inside within my heart.
The side of me that cares a lot.
The grief that hides inside entangled with
The fear and love that scares me till the day is dark.
Never will they understand the way I feel no matter how they try.

Sometimes, trying to relate creates more problems than it

solves. One teenager wrote angrily about his parents' attempts to be involved in his life.

Dear Rodney,
If my parents knew the things they do that get on my nerves,
then they wouldn't do them because they love me enough to do
that for me. My mom is always trying to be a joker about every-
thing, but it's never funny. Even when I ask her to stop she won't
because she thinks it's funny. Then I get mad and start yelling
and then everybody gets mad. Then I get in trouble for some-
thing that my mom starts and gets on my nerves real bad.
My dad used to go everywhere with the youth of the church,
which I understood. But now he's not one of the volunteers any-
more, but he still goes to all the youth events, and I can't do
anything I want to because he's always there to tell me I can't
do it.
And I can't stand the fact that my dad gives in to my mom all
the time. Like if I want to do something my dad won't give me an
answer. He'll just say to ask my mom.
I hope they can understand these things if I ever have the guts
to tell them. Then they can stop, and I can stop getting so mad
at them. And we could all love each other more.
Tommy

Sometimes the problem is a temporary setback as the teenager flexes her developmental muscles of independence. That stage will pass, as this mother hopes.

Rodney,
Sometimes I feel confused. I want Jenny to talk to me, but I'm re-
ally afraid of what she'd say if she did. So I'm angry at her be-
cause she won't talk, but I fear what she would say if she did.
When she won't talk to me, I feel rejected, like she doesn't need
me—or worse, doesn't want me to be a part of her life.
When she was younger, she used to crawl on my lap and we'd
laugh and talk. When she was hurt, she came running up to me
for me to comfort her. Somehow, I'm afraid I've done something
to ruin that special feeling of trust and love we used to share.
I see Jenny with other people, like her friends, and she seems so

relaxed and free. But at home, she seems so tense. Sometimes she snaps at me or her brother or her sister for the smallest thing. I wish she could be relaxed and free around us. I've read some books on adolescents, and they all say that kids need to become separate from their families during this time. I guess that makes sense, but I wish my heart understood it better. It still feels like rejection to me. And I wonder if I've driven her away by something I've said or done.

I've tried to talk to her like we used to, but she turns cold. I've tried to talk to her like a friend, but we aren't friends. Other parents tell me just to wait, that it'll get better. I hope they're right.

Margaret

But sometimes the problem isn't developmental. It isn't a stage. The child doesn't communicate because the parents have proven they are untrustworthy and unsafe. This adolescent felt betrayed when she mustered the courage to tell her parents the hard, unvarnished truth.

Dear Rodney,

I had a happy childhood until I turned eight and began going across the street to my aunt's house to be babysat during the summer. My cousin, who was five or so years older, took advantage of my love and total trust and began molesting me. He told me that if I told anyone it would ruin the whole family and it'd be all my fault. The abuse continued for a little over a year. I began to cry each time I had to have a babysitter, but I couldn't tell my parents why.

Finally, I told my mother. She told my father. I realize how hurtful and painful it was for them that their nephew was hurting their little girl, but to this day I question the way they handled it. My father told my cousin in private to stay away from me, and then my parents told me to forget it, move on, and never tell anyone because it would break up the whole family.

I felt so abandoned—as if they didn't care about me as much as the well-being of my cousin. He got away with a slap on the wrist! I put the pain away, deep inside, and put up a wall. I have a hard time trusting. And I was terribly confused about men in general.

When I was fifteen, a sophomore in high school, I realized that I didn't know what my destination would be if I died. In tears, I called my pastor and he prayed with me over the phone. On the day before Thanksgiving 1992 at 8:00 P.M., I gave my heart to Jesus.

For a few months, I determined to be a good Christian. I worked hard to "walk the walk." I failed in the middle of July 1993. I was dating a non-Christian guy who I did not know well. Deep down inside, I wanted to be "protected" because I felt abandoned still. I was stupid enough to do anything to keep this guy. Knowing full well that premarital sex is a sin and that I would regret it later, I believed him when he said he loved me, and I gave him my virginity. We were together again a few weeks later. When school began in my junior year, he ditched me. I was heartbroken, ashamed, and feeling hopelessly abandoned again.

Instead of repenting, I latched onto another guy and made the same mistake, then he dumped me. The episode was repeated Spring Break of this year with a different guy, a Christian who told me he'd NEVER leave me. Then he did.

In the past four months, I have lived every day with the remorse and feelings of filthiness. It was so hard that I couldn't tell my parents. They can never know. It would break their hearts. The worst part was the tearing at my conscience by the Holy Spirit. I thought I'd messed up too much, gone too far, and that God could never, ever forgive me. I was just not worth it. I tried and tried to reason it out in my head, but my heart just hurt.

Last summer, I went to a church camp. Each message seemed to be shooting right at me. For the first time in years, I felt the Holy Spirit move. I learned that Jesus can forgive even the messed-up Christian, and my heart just broke. In the middle of that week at camp, I gave Jesus all my burdens as well as complete control of my life. The minute I did that, the most beautiful peace filled my heart. I felt like singing and raising my hands to Jesus—and I did! At the same time, I became a spiritual virgin, because God forgave me. And I tried to forgive my cousin.

I cannot tell my parents this, but I forgive them and I love them with all my heart. They can never understand the pain I've been through and the contrast of that to the joy I feel now.
Mom and Dad, you've done well raising me. My mistakes are my own, but I'm back in God's will now. I love you.

Michele

"Did you ever stop to consider that adolescents *learned* to stop communicating with their parents?" a friend told a group of concerned parents at a seminar. "And they learned this from their parents."

The people in the class seemed to rise as one in protest. "What do you mean?" several of them demanded in a menacing tone.

"I mean that many parents give very clear messages to their kids: messages that it is safe to be honest about your thoughts and feelings or messages that it is very unsafe."

The parents looked confused.

"Oh, I'm not talking about an open declaration. I'm talking about nonverbal communication and parents' reactions to the signals kids put out." For the rest of the session, he described the parents' "nonverbals and reactions," which teach teenagers either to continue to talk or to keep their opinions to themselves.

Some of the signals parents give kids are in their verbal and nonverbal responses to:

- kids' successes
- kids' failures
- kids' music
- kids' friends
- kids' clothes
- kids' attitudes toward homework and school
- how kids handle conflict
- how kids treat adults
- how kids treat siblings

The parents' primary mistake is in valuing control above all else. Certainly, control and order are important, but they aren't of primary importance except in life-threatening situations. Communication and understanding are more important. When kids experiment with new behaviors, attitudes, and perspectives, many parents feel threatened and instantly react negatively instead of using the situation as an opportunity for communication. These reactions shut down the teenagers. They tell the teens they shouldn't be open, and they should keep things from their parents because they can't be trusted. They learn to withhold their feelings and opinions.

Some people (adults and children) have very low thresholds for stress. They react to virtually any perceived loss of control. Others have higher thresholds and stay calm under considerably more stress. Sooner or later, though, the tolerance level is broken, and they react in order to regain control and punish the one who disrupted the equilibrium of life. Instead of responding by listening, communicating, setting realistic expectations, and continuing to maintain a safe, healthy environment, both types of parents teach their teenage children they aren't safe by:

- *Condemning*—"I told you so!", name calling, glaring, disgust, bringing up the error again and again.
- *Punishing*—going beyond healthy discipline to revenge themselves and make the teenager pay dearly for the error.
- *Exploding*—yelling, throwing things, hitting, cursing.
- *Withdrawing*—retreating from the adolescent emotionally or physically either as punishment or to insulate themselves from the conflict (or both).
- *Fixing*—jumping in to solve the teenager's problems; not allowing her to think and make decisions for herself; robbing her of dignity and responsibility.
- *Joking*—attempting to lower the level of tension with humor.
- *Acting sarcastic*—using humor at another's expense, actually intended to take revenge on the victim.
- *Taking the blame*—attempting to resolve conflict by being a "blame sponge" so the other person won't get upset at having to bear responsibility.
- *Avoiding the issue*—talking about every issue except the one

which needs to be addressed; acting like the problem doesn't exist.

- *Demanding change*—insisting that the teenager change unilaterally instead of listening, communicating, and working out realistic expectations for each person.
- *Expanding the problem*—overreacting to one problem by assuming that the teenager is at fault in many other areas of life too.
- *Medicating to escape*—attempting to avoid the pain of family conflict by taking drugs or drinking alcohol.

I want to include some letters from some teenagers who probably don't feel they can communicate these things to their parents. They are full of anger and despair.

Dear Rodney,
Since my mother married my step-father, everything has gone down hill. My mom and dad got devorced when I was two years old and my older sister was five. My dad remarried when I was around seven years old, and my mom remarried when I was nine. My mom's second marriage was the total pitts. He moved into our family after my mom knowing him for a little over six months, and me a little over six days. Every time I spoke to this man, he always put my sister and I down. (I even tried one time to leave notes in her sweaters that asked her, "Mama, please do not marry him. He called me some really bad things while you were not home.")
I just wish she would have listened to me. She thought I was joking, so she gave him this note and he confronted me. All I could do was cry. This man totally ruined our lives. He had an ex wife and three kids. Two of them moved in with us. This new family would not have been so bad if they were not such bad influences. For example, one was an alcoholic and drug user and the other was a collect-a-maniac.
I was torn from my mother because of these people we had living in our home. After this marriage, we moved an hour away from my home town to my mom's home town. Five years after my mom and step-father were married, my sister, my mom, and I

left. He was committing adultery and my mom could not handle it. The worst thing was that he would treat my family like we were nothing. I hated him for this. He would always be on my case about everything and still I hated him. I felt that I was all alone because of him.

Since we have moved away from him, 99 percent of everything has changed. I started going to church. I felt I needed something to fill the empty spots in my life. After that, I became more out-going. But this wore off within about three months. I was with the wrong crowd, and the only way I felt I could do anything was to drink and get drunk and smoke to get high. I felt good when I did that.

The worst thing for me to get threw was all the times my mother told me to clean the house. I would do what she asked me to do, but when she came home she didn't even say anything about it. It hurt me so bad. I would work all day on what she told me to do and I was not respected at all. My main point is: People will come and go no matter how much you love or hate them.

Rachel

Dear Rodney,

Thank you for speaking at our school. What you were saying re-ally made a great impact on a young teenager like me. I'm only in the ninth grade. I just wanted to break down in tears. I can't imagine how much it takes to get in front of all these people and tell them about your life story and other people's life story. There's a lot of things that my "mom" doesn't know. She gets mad at me because when my x-step-sister came over this past weekend, I locked the door so I could talk to her about some things. Well, my mom has the urge to sneak up on me and listen to my conversations with whoever. Well, I locked the door, and turned up the radio to block things out. She tried opening the door while we were talking. She started banging on the door and saying, "Unlock this —— door!" Well, I did and she asked me why did I have it locked? I told her because me and Kay (my x-step-sister) were talking about some things, and I didn't want anyone to know about. Well then she screamed at me and said, "How come you have secrets from me! I don't have any from you! I'm your Mom!"

That made me really mad and sad at the same time. That same night my boyfriend came over. I lost my virginity that same night. It's not like I haven't wanted to have sex with him, it's just that my mom, as you know, listened in.

I finally confronted her about listening in on my business. She then denide it. But later in the conversation she finally said, "That's a mother's job to do that, and when you have a child, you'll do the same thing."

It's like if I tell my mom what I really do, she gets mad. Well I have been smoking "pot" but not very often. I only do it when I want to have nothing on my mind. So I don't have to worry about things until my high goes away.

I wish I could travel somewhere with you, Rodney, just to see what things are like.

Gretchen

Messages are communicated in three ways: by physical touch, verbally, and with gestures. Physical touch can take the form of hugs or hitting; verbal messages can be talking and listening or yelling; gestures can be looks of concern, raised eyebrows, hand movements, or glares. Actually, tone of voice, gestures, and expressions communicate our message far more strongly and clearly than our words alone. A teenager can hear the words, "I care about you," from a scowling, glaring mother, and conclude, "You sure don't seem to care. You look like you want to bite my head off!" But if the message is communicated with a tender voice and a look of genuine love, the words will match the medium and the message will get through.

Parents often make the mistake of assuming their children are just like them—chips off the old block. That assumption may be true to a great extent, but God designed our children to be very different from us in personality, temperament, and giftedness. Some of us want our children to live out our own dreams—to be the success we never quite were and avoid the stupid mistakes we made. It is fine and good to want them to do well, but we need to recognize their individuality and let them develop their own sense of identity and direction in life. One father came to this conclusion very slowly and painfully.

Dear Rodney,

I thought I understood my son, Jody. I thought he was the same kind of kid I was when I was his age, with the same desires and goals and wants and needs. I guess I was imposing my views on him because last week he told me that he and I are different people with different dreams. He was really mad at me.

I've seen Jody get mad like this before, but he never said why. I sure didn't know it was this. It's a good thing, I guess, that he had the guts to tell me how he felt. Otherwise, I'd never have figured it out, and I'd have kept expecting him to "follow in my footsteps."

I feel pretty down about it all. Down because I didn't understand, because he has felt pressure from me for a long time but didn't feel the freedom to say anything, and down because he doesn't want to be like his old man. He loves his music and his art work. He said he doesn't care about sports and business like me. He's a really gifted artist. He's won some awards at school and everything, but I never dreamed he wanted to do that for the rest of his life.

Now I've got to make some changes. I've got to understand what makes him tick and stop believing he's just like me. He's a good kid. He'll do alright whatever he does.

Thanks.

Bill

No matter how tense the relationship, communication can begin and grow deep and strong. Some families have "family conferences" every week and allow each family member three minutes to say anything they want without being interrupted. I suggest you try this. You may want to do it one-on-one the first time so the teenagers can learn to trust you and your intentions. Begin by asking questions like, "What do you like best about our family?" and "What are two things you wish I'd do differently?" You may have very different perceptions and solutions, but the goal is good communication. Problem identification and solving can come after the communication is established.

Listen carefully to whatever is said without reacting, and thank each person for being honest. That will be a good start in developing a deeper, stronger relationship with your teenager.

Changing poor communication habits is often difficult, but it is well worth the time and emotional energy required. God wants to give strength, forgiveness, and love to mend strained and broken relationships if we will let Him. But of course, for relationships to truly mend, both parties must be willing to learn to forgive and love again. A lady wrote me about how her relationship with her daughter began to improve.

Dear Rodney,

I didn't want to hear what Sarah said, but it was the beginning of healing and hope in our family. For the past few years, the tension had been building. Frank was transferred, my mother died, my father became depressed and we didn't know how to help him, and Sarah became a teenager. Any one of those would have been enough stress, but together, well, we didn't handle it very well.

I had to go back to Pittsburgh several times in the months before Mom died. I wanted to be with her, and I wanted to comfort my Dad. After she died and he got depressed, we asked him to come live with us because my brother didn't want to take him to his house. My brother lives a lot closer, but he's too selfish to help Dad. When Dad moved in with us, he was a different person than the man we had known. He was so quiet. He sat and watched TV mostly. He never smiled or laughed.

And Sarah was in the eighth grade that year. Looking back on it, I can see how she would feel neglected, but we were doing absolutely all we knew to do. But we could have been a little more discerning about how all the changes were affecting our family. Sarah became quiet around us. It happened so gradually, and we were so preoccupied with all the other things going on, we hardly noticed. By the time she was a sophomore in high school, it was like she was a stranger living in our house. By that time, Dad had moved back home. My brother had agreed to see about him more, and I was less angry at my brother. But by then, Sarah only gave us one-word or one-phrase responses. She talked very openly with other adults and with her friends, but not with her father and me, or with her older sister. When I finally noticed there was a problem, I thought we could work it out pretty easily. After all, all she had to do was talk.

But I was wrong. It wasn't that easy at all. Sarah said she was fine, and when I pressed her, she got angry and told me to leave her alone. A couple of months went by like this. I looked for opportunities, but Sarah was now running from any attempts to get below the surface. Finally, I talked to our youth pastor, Phil. He said he would try to talk to her and see what happened.

Phil is great with the kids. He has their trust. He waited for the right time, then one day on a bus trip to an amusement park, he sat on a bench with Sarah and slowly began to talk to her about her feelings which had become buried. After talking about some of the rides and the boys spending a fortune trying to win basketballs, Phil said something like, "Tell me about your family, Sarah. Didn't your grandfather live with you for a while? That seems like it would be pretty hard." And he waited for her to respond.

She began slowly, telling him that he was right. It was hard. He followed up and expressed how he would have felt if his family had moved, his grandmother had died, his grandfather moved in with them, and the stress level in the family had sky-rocketed when he needed stability in junior high. Sarah tapped into his honesty, and said, "Yeah, I felt pretty lonely. Left out."

They sat for a minute. Then she volunteered, "But mom and dad don't understand." Wisely, Phil didn't tell her that I was dying to talk to her about her feelings. Phil just nodded. "That hurts, too," he told her.

Over the next couple of months, Phil looked for good opportunities to talk to Sarah. They laughed and talked about a lot of things. Sometimes in groups, sometimes just the two of them. As Sarah opened up about her feelings of abandonment and her anger at us, Phil told her, "You know, I bet your parents can tell you feel that way." Sarah told him she doubted it. A few days later, I was looking at pictures in an old album, and Sarah came over to look. We came to some pictures of the year my mother died. I said something like, "We don't have many pictures of that year. And none of these are very happy." Then I asked her, "Did you feel sad or lonely that year, Sarah?"

That was the start for us to communicate. She told me she had felt very sad and alone. I didn't press it, then a few seconds later, she said, "Did you know I felt that way, Mom?" I told her that I didn't realize it then, but I did later. That was all we said at that time, but it opened the door for us to move slowly and carefully into each other's lives. Sarah still is a little withdrawn, but when she wants to talk, she is deep and perceptive. I've apologized for not understanding how all the stress affected her. She didn't really want to talk about it. That was a little too deep for her at the moment. I hope we can continue. I feel like I have my daughter back.

Sincerely,
Carol

Reflection/Discussion Questions

1. How did you feel as you read the letters in this chapter?
2. Did you feel you could talk to your parents when you were a teenager? Why or why not?
3. What are some verbal messages you give your teenager?
4. What are some nonverbal messages?
5. What particular circumstances seem to repeatedly trigger negative messages toward your teenager? (For example: bad grades, being messy, being late, loud music, bad choices about friends, etc.)
6. Plan a family conference to promote communication.
   - What are your goals for the conference?
   - How will it be conducted?
   - What are the ground rules?
   - What is the time limit?
   - When will it occur?
   - How can you prepare for it emotionally?
   - What will be the next step after the conference?

PART 2

If My Parents Knew . . .

... How Uptight I Feel

Many teenagers live every day with a high level of tension. Family stress, miscommunication, gang violence, drugs, teen pregnancy, peer rejection, and heartache seem to lurk around every corner. Just the idea that these things are possible makes them feel uptight all the time. Many kids feel their parents add to their stress levels.

> Dear Rodney,
> Maybe they'd understand. Its bound to make me uptight when I have three hours of homework every night. And it makes me uptight when my parents drill me into a sweat about friends, my girlfriend, sex, drugs, and other important issues. They need to be talked about, but my parents could give me a chance to talk, and just give me some space. They always ask why I am so uptight, well if they were in my place they'd understand and maybe they'd step back a half step and give me some room to breathe.
>
> Mark

> Dear Rodney,
> My parents think I have more than twenty-four hours in a day. After I get home from school I practically have to go again doing

my homework. Then I have to do all my chores before anything else, and we have a big family so that takes a long time. Usually until I need to get to sleep. Every once in a while I'd like a break, to watch TV or sleep. I'm so tired all the time. The pressures from school and my parents can be unbearable. I don't have thirty hours a day.

Rhonda

Many of the teenagers who talk to me tell me their parents don't understand them and are too strict.

Dear Rodney,
I love my parents, but they are too strict. They won't let me go or do anything with my friends. And they make me clean my room everyday. I like my room a little messy. They also always get mad at me when I'm always on the phone, but I have nothing else to do. And some of my friends from church that I never get to see because they don't go to my school, I like to talk to them and see how they are doing. I wish my parents knew this.

Paula

Dear Rodney,
I don't think that parents really understand the pressures and temptations that teenagers go through these days. At least mine don't. They can try to understand and care about what I do, but they just can't. They don't face the same situations now that teenagers do. When they were teens, they had to go up against different pressures and have different confrontations. They may have had similar thoughts and feelings, but it's just not the same today. They cannot understand fully the pressures and temptations I feel.

Patrick

And some teenagers tell me their parents expect them to be perfect. The teens don't seem to mind expectations, even high expectations, as long as they aren't unrealistic and they receive some affirmation for trying hard.

Rodney,

If my dad knew how much he makes me mad when I do good with my grades, homework, chores, and stay out of trouble, he never lets me know or shows he is proud. I try my best and all I get is more trouble. I mean he expects me to be perfect. I make A's and B's do all my chores and he acts like something is missing, like I'm not good enough. I don't know, I just want to hear, "that's good Judie, you're doing well."

Judie

Dear Rodney,

As a teenager, I feel extreme pressures to do my best in school, sports, and anything else. The pressure adults place on teenagers, whether they know it or not, makes us feel nervous, scared, or even angry. If parents and teachers would just ease up a little, a lot of people would feel a lot better.

Jeffrey

Many of the stresses teenagers experience are the result of family crises they can't control. In too many families, conflict is seldom, if ever, resolved. The tension turns into anger and the anger into bitterness. Divorce is often a culprit for creating emotional distress, but the divorce itself is only the surface issue. Underneath are dysfunctional dynamics which erode and shatter trust in relationships.

Dear Rodney,

My family hurt me when my mom kept telling me she was going to get a divorce. My mom and dad had been fighting very often. It would hurt me to see them fight, but I didn't want them to split up. After their fights my mom would keep telling me that she wanted a divorce. During that time I cried myself to sleep many nights. I am not an emotional person. I don't cry very often. Something has to hurt alot to cause me to cry. It even grew to the point if a divorce would stop the fighting I was about willing for it to happen. I prayed about it alot. I can gladly say that my parents are still together. They don't fight as much, and especially in front of my sister and myself. I never told my

mom how much it hurt me. I tried to hide it, and I think I was successful.

Still another way I have been hurt is by my mom. I have a sister
that is twelve, so we are five years apart. She and I don't get
along, but that's another story. With my sister being the baby
of the family she is treated like a baby. My mom allows her to
use the title "baby" as an escape and advantage. My mom allows her to do things I have never been allowed to do. Even to
the point if my sister doesn't want to go to church sometime,
then its okay. My mom makes me go on to church. Most the
time I want to go. A few times I have been tired and have wanted
to sleep in and just go to preaching. My mom made me got to
both Sunday School and preaching. It has made me a stronger
Christian, but I just don't understand why I am treated differently from my sister. I am her daughter too. I don't drink, smoke,
or have sex. I do what my mom wants, so why am I different? I
love both my mom and sister very much, but it hurts to be
treated like that.

There have been many other hurts. These are the main ones
that stand out in my mind. I love my family very much. I pray and
God gives me strength and peace. I don't see how people without Christ can make it in the world.

Priscilla

Professor, author, and speaker Dr. Archibald Hart has written
best-selling books on the stress we experience in our society.[1] His
studies reveal that we live in a society which creates a very high
level of tension in all of us. This tension is so pervasive, we don't
even notice it any more. It has become normal. We run to the
grocery store. We run to work, where we have to produce "or
else." We run our children to practices and games and recitals. We
run to church. We hurry to spend time with God. We spend time
on the freeways trying to get to our next appointment. We eat fast
food and go through the drive through at the bank. When our job
changes, we move a thousand miles away and try to rebuild a
sense of stability and meaningful relationships in the middle of
another hectic environment. And about the time we feel estab-

lished, we move again, somebody dies, or a close friend moves away.

All of this is extremely difficult for adults, but it is *devastating* for young people who desperately need security, stability, and strong relationships to help them cope with cataclysmic hormonal and developmental changes. They have enough normal adolescent problems to worry about without the added stresses and hectic pace of our times. Many of our teenage sons and daughters feel stressed, but it has become so normal to feel this way, they don't even realize the problem. And we can't help them because it has become normal for us too.

The answer is probably not a return to the slower, more focused life of the ninteenth century (after all, they didn't even have antihistamines or television). But parents would be wise to take a hard look at the pace and stress levels of their lives, as well as their children's, and take some steps to slow down and enjoy life before it passes them by. Some parents, however, try to remember the "good ole days" in ways that actually put more pressure on their kids.

Dear Rodney,
I wish my parents knew how it felt to be a part of my generation. I believe they would realize how easy they actually had it. Growing up now is much harder than everyone sees it to be. I may have to go through some things similar to what my parents went through, but there are many problems that I have they never had to face. There are problems that I have deep inside that I don't talk to my parents about.
In the time period my parents grew up they didn't have to worry as much about drugs or alcohol. They didn't have to worry about walking out onto the sidewalk and being shot at or having someone push them into drugs. I am thankful to God that I live in a small town where there isn't much crime. I worry about being in a situation one day where I may not be able to side step the bullet or say "no" to smoking a joint.
My parents talk about having to walk to school ten miles a day barefoot in the snow. That's their way of saying I have it easy. I have news for them. We don't. Sometimes I lie awake at night

and wonder what I will do if I am rejected by my friends or I am offered a joint. I pray my children do not have to face the same trials I face today and if they do I pray they will feel as if they can talk to me or their father about it.

I believe that if my parents knew about the trials of my life they would be a little more understanding when I am having a bad day.

Janie

Some adolescents stagger under a heavy load of expectations. Sometimes these expectations are self-imposed. Sometimes they are the product of well-meaning parents. And sometimes, they stem from miscommunication. This young man wrote me about the pressure he feels to be a successful lawyer.

Dear Rodney,

My Mom and Dad put a lot of pressure on me. I try so hard every day to win their approval, but it does so little good. Don't get me wrong, some pressure is good. It's made me start making those grades; but somewhere there has to be a breaking point.

I have been told that I am expected to become a successful lawyer to be able to support my family. I am to be the one that will change my family's life, fulfill their dreams, make life easier, and doing it as a lawyer.

But I believe God wants me to be a missionary. How can I tell Mom and Dad. They will come unglued! How can I tell them so they will understand. What can I do? My life has been one big pleasure party for everyone to suck from. There have been times when I wanted to give up and leave home because I didn't want to tell them that God wants me to be a missionary.

This is a continual worry and hurt for me and my parents are Christian.

Franklin

Another stress factor for adolescents is comparison. It is human nature to compare, but teenagers carry this tendency to the extreme. They look to their peers for identity and security. They endlessly analyze their clothes, hair, complexion, performance, and especially their standing in the peer group, to see if they are okay. The trap is that no place in this pecking order provides security. Even those at the top fear somebody else coming along to threaten their position. Failure (and dreaded ostracism) lurks around every corner.

This somewhat normal part of adolescence is compounded by the media portrayals of "the perfect teen"—a phantom who has everything: great hair, flawless complexion, a tremendous body, the finest in-style clothes, and the fawning of the adoring masses. Virtually every commercial targeted to young people presents this image of the supremely attractive and popular teenager. "All you have to do is buy this product!" It is no wonder that many teens feel out of control, awkward, unattractive, and unpopular— or at least they fear feeling this way.

Another cause of stress in teenagers is repressed anger in their parents, which is often unleashed by alcohol or drugs. Kids usually bear the brunt of the violence because they are least likely to threaten the one who is out of control.

Dear Rodney,
My family is really violent. My mom drinks and loses control and yells at me. My half-brother was put in jail for fighting. My grand-father's daughter got killed, and then he started drinking and he got really mad and started beating on me. My grandmother told him that if he ever laid a hand on me again, we'd be gone. My grandmother and I finally moved out and he kept calling her and pestering her. She finally met somebody at church that I picked out for her. He was a fine kinda guy. I got to know him really well. I've tried to talk to my grandfather but he just cusses me out. My grandfather doesn't really love me. My life's been like a wreck. It's been a total hell. I don't know how to deal with all the pain all the time. I don't know how to deal with it. I've come through a lot of it.
I've got a boyfriend now. He makes me feel close and special. We're doing some things—but I just want somebody to love me.
Rita

Most of us can remember a defining moment of our high school years when a close friend—or several friends—was senselessly killed in an accident. The memory of these tragedies adds to the amorphous sense of stress in teenagers. I don't think I'll ever forget the day I spoke to about 2500 high school students at an assembly in Virginia Beach. After I spoke, some of them wanted to talk with me. They shared their hurts and hopes. The last one in line was Melanie, a beautiful, dark-haired junior. Melanie sat next to me in the gym bleachers and after a sigh, she burst into tears.

She said haltingly, "Rodney, I feel so guilty. My best friend, Beth, is dead." Over the next few minutes, Melanie told me a story that is tragically repeated thousands of times each year in communities all across our country.

It all began one afternoon when Beth and I were at a stop light just down the street from here. A brand new 300ZX pulled up next to us, and Beth noticed the guy driving it. He was really good-looking. She whispered to me to take a look at him, and then she rolled down her window to talk to him.

Rodney, we didn't even know who this guy was, but Beth was flirting with him! He invited us to meet him at a bar that night at the beach. When the light turned green, he took off and I laughed. But Beth wanted to go meet him. I thought she was insane! But she talked me into it.

We met him at about ten o'clock. He bought us a few drinks, then we left the bar and rode around in his car. We laughed and talked for a while, and then he asked me to go home with him. Beth was too drunk to drive her own car, so I suggested that I drive her car to her house. We'd let her off there, and then he and I could go to his house.

On the way to Beth's house, this guy was going way too fast! He must have been going over one hundred miles an hour over the bridge. I tried to follow them, but I lost them. When I got over the top of the bridge, I saw there had just been a tremendous wreck! Their car had swerved into the oncoming lane and they had a head-on crash! The car was on fire. There was no way to get Beth out.

Melanie buried her head in her hands and wept. After a minute, she gathered herself and continued.

"You know, Beth's death really had an effect on all the students at the school. Lots of us were used to getting wasted on weekends, but that stopped—for some people anyway."

Melanie looked puzzled and angry. "You know what really bugs me?" she asked. "What bugs me is that after only a couple of weeks, a lot of people were back to getting wasted every weekend, like nothing had ever happened at all."

"And you?" I asked.

"No. Not me. I won't ever be the same."

Many of us live in suburban America. We see the tragedies of teen pregnancies on television, and occasionally we are horrified to find it has happened in our own communities. Similarly, we see news coverage of violence on the local news each night, and we hope we will be spared the trauma of becoming a victim. But millions of young people live every day in a world where teen pregnancies and senseless violence are the norm. Fear and heartache are also the norm. This teenager wrote me about her horror of being abused.

Dear Rodney,

Last year my boyfriend started drinking a lot and doing cocaine with it, and we finally broke up because he started beating on my baby, Andy. Andy is only three months old. My boyfriend had this bad habit when he was high on booze and cocaine, he got really violent. He stuck a knife in my arm, a three inch blade. It went all the way through and broke my bone. I have pins in my arm bone now. He's in jail.

He wasn't like that when I first started going out with him. He was nice. He sent me roses and flowers and then he went to college and got weird. I was eighteen when I had Andy. I wouldn't give him up and I wouldn't have an abortion cause my mom does not believe in that. But I love Andy to death. I won't let my boyfriend near him, but he's in jail now, so he can't get near him. I didn't marry him. I wasn't going through with that. He tried to kill his present girlfriend, so he's in jail on two counts now. At first I didn't want to have the baby because of the circumstances under which I was having it. But now I love Andy. I wouldn't give him up for anything. He's my baby. Well, my boyfriend's mom keeps Andy during the day while I go to school. She's really divorced herself from her son, and she keeps the baby during the day.

My boyfriend and I broke up when I was one month pregnant with Andy. I started dating another guy and we've been together now about ten months. He loves Andy to death. He doesn't drink or smoke. He's perfect!

Nobody here at school really knows about the baby. I didn't come to school at all last year. My best friend and my mom, they're the only ones who know.

Jessica

Another young woman tells her story of abuse, heartache, and desperation.

Dear Rodney,
I was raped when I was over at my friends house she was a sleep. Her boyfriend came in and raped me. It happened a second time when the man my mother was seeing tried to. I told my father and he called Family Servis Center, and I told them about it. They brought a doll out, and they told me to show them so they could understand what happen. It was horrible. The third time my teacher put his hand on my butt and touch somewhere he was not sopost to touch. But he did anyway.

My mother wanted me to be a boy. My name was going to be John Wayne. But I turned out to be a little girl. My name is Ginger. I had a sister but she died. She was only three months old. I miss her right now. I love my sister dearly. Her name is Angela. She would be eight years old now if she had lived.

My mother has done drugs. I don't know if she still does. She told me she never would touch it again. One day I walked in her room and there she was smoking it. I sat down on the floor. Why mother? What did I ever do to my mother to make her do this?

*We got into a big fuss and I said something about it. And she
goes "what are you talking about?"
I went and got it and throwed it in the toilet. She said "what
about your smoking?" (I had got caught four times) and I said
"yes, I know." I admitted it. I know I'd did wrong, and I know I
should hadn't try it because it hurt me a lot.
My dad was in a car axodent and he all most died. I love him
alot. My step sister said my father kissed her, and touched her
in places. I didn't believe her. I'll alway be a daddy's girl. I love my
father. But if it is true, I will not see him as my role motel, or a
person that I look up to.
I pray almost every night for my sister. She does not belive in
God. I think she is that way because she is afrade of him. I love
her alot. I don't want me or her to go to hell or any of my family.
When my mother is doing drugs, she hit me sometimes. I felt like
she hated me. I hope she comes closer to God.
My aunt died. Her name is Beverly and her baby name is Ginger.
Named after me. They were coming home and a big truck hit
them and made me feel so bad. The baby looked like a doll.*
Ginger

Teenagers have a lot to be uptight about these days! An important part of growing up is learning which stresses need to be avoided and which ones must be endured so that we learn from them. This distinction is not an easy one. Many of the stresses young people (and adults) experience are the natural consequences of seemingly innocent decisions. Staying up until two o'clock in the morning to talk on the phone may seem important to your daughter, but when she falls asleep in class the next day, the teacher probably won't be too sympathetic about her need to know the latest social news.

The Scriptures are full of admonitions, encouragement, and warnings about wisdom in our priorities, relationships, desires, thoughts, and our use of time and money. Some of the stresses we experience are the result of others' decisions, such as a parent's divorce or a friend's anger, but many are the products of our own misguided choices. Talk to your teenager about these important issues in a way that is positive and comfortable for both of you. (That means, don't react when he says something off the wall! He may just want to see if you will really listen to him.) And help your teenager find a youth group where kids learn true wisdom for the crucial decisions they are making.

Some questions you can ask your teen are:

- What are the most fun things you did this week?
- What people or things disappointed you the most?
- If your friends could ask God one question, what would it be?
- What are some of the biggest stresses in the lives of people in your class? How are they dealing with these stresses?
- What are some differences in what people at your school think and what God thinks about . . .
  - . . . status
  - . . . money
  - . . . sex and dating
  - . . . school work
  - . . . going to college
  - . . . drugs
  - . . . racism
  - . . . anything else you or your teenager thinks is important
- What can you do about the stresses in your life? Which ones can be avoided by better decisions? Which ones do you need to learn and grow from?

Many people try to escape life's stresses by using drugs, television, sex, food, friends, or some other way. But when we can't avoid stress, we can learn from it. God can use the difficulties in our lives to shape our character and make us better people. In fact, the results can be so positive, Paul told the believers in Rome that they could actually rejoice in their problems!

. . . we also glory in tribulations, knowing that tribulation produces perseverance; and perseverance, character; and character, hope. Now hope does not disappoint, because the love of God has been poured out in our hearts by the Holy Spirit who was given to us. (Rom. 5:3-5)

Some stresses can be avoided. Some are inevitable. Help your teenager understand the difference and gain wisdom.

Reflection/Discussion Questions

1. List ten factors which increase your stress level.
2. List ten factors which increase your teenager's stress level.
3. Which of these (in questions 1 and 2) are controllable? Which are unavoidable?
4. How do the following contribute to your teenager's stress?
   - the media
   - school
   - comparison with peers
   - hormones
   - family problems
   - money
   - appearance
   - athletics
   - other
5. Examine the questions listed on page 34. Would it be good for you to discuss these with your teenager? If so, when? Where?

CHAPTER 4

. . . How Much I Want to Be Somebody

The home environment helps shape a young person's sense of identity—for better or worse.

Dear Rodney,

I'm angry about many things in life that have something to do with my parents. Things like what I like to do, decision making, and many other things.

My parents rarely ever let me do things that I like to do. They tell me where I'm going to go and how long I'm staying. I, myself, like to go skating with my friends. But my parents hardly ever let me go. When I ask them why they say, "Are they christians?" I tell them "yes" but they still hardly ever let me go.

In decision making, my parents don't seem to trust me and that makes me angry. For example, they never like any of my new friends. They always try to "hook me up" with some of my old friends. Not that there is anything wrong with them. I just don't know them any more.

Some other things that make me angry towards my parents; They always bother me by never give me a little privacy. They also spoil my brother and sister but when I need or want some they say "no." But when my brother and sister ask for something they get it. I don't think that is fair and I think they should be told about what I feel but I'm scared of them. I am very angry towards my parents and at least want an explanation sometimes. All I've asked for in the past is to understand my parents motives and reasons.

Hillary

"Who am I?"
"Why am I here?"
These are questions young people ask. These are questions which demand answers!

In earlier years, children look to their parents for their identity. In their book *Getting Unstuck,* Robert McGee and Pat Springle state that parents are "mirrors" which reflect the value and image of the child.

A child determines things such as his value, abilities, and worth as a person by his parents' attitudes and actions toward him. If parents are loving and kind, provide a safe home environment, and encourage growth toward individual responsibility, then they're very good mirrors of a child's worth. Generally, children in these homes grow up with a healthy sense of identity, able to give and receive love, and willing to take responsibility for life's tasks. But like carnival mirrors, parental "mirrors" can be distorted. The more distorted the mirror, the more distorted the image. If the child perceives a reflection of being unsafe, unlovable, or worthless, he begins to develop problems with his identity, relationships, and level of responsibility (either too much or too little). . . . The reason we thought the mirrors in the "Haunted House" were funny was that we had other accurate mirrors with which to compare our reflections. But if someone has only one distorted mirror to look into every day, he may believe that it is himself—not the mirror—which is distorted.[1]

In the adolescent years, teens change mirrors. They no longer look to their parents for their identity. Instead, they look to their peers. The choice of peers in this period of their lives is more important than almost any other choice. Their identity, sense of direction, and sphere of relationships will form the basis for the most important decisions they will make in their lives: who they will marry, who they will serve, and what their purpose in life will be. Most people make these three critical choices during the middle or latter part of adolescence.

Some young people enter their teen years with clear, positive images of themselves. Others, however, begin these difficult years carrying a load of self-doubt and shame. Woe to those who are emotionally crippled at the starting gate! The strong, healthy teenager naturally experiments with new ideas and behaviors. She questions authority and learns to think for herself. If she begins with self-doubt and shame, these experiments and questions may not be tempered by reason and stability. Instead, they are exacerbated by defiance, defensiveness, and a drive to withdraw from risk or take every risk in order to prove herself. But no matter how well she performs, it's not good enough. There's always somebody a little bit better, smarter, better-looking, or more gifted. And even if she climbs to the top, she lives with the fear of failing and falling back.

Most people who struggle with perfectionism focus on one particular area of their lives. Just one. That's enough. But some people feel driven to be the best in virtually every area. Recently I met a high school senior who was the Student Body President and the head cheerleader on the varsity squad. She had a perfect 4.0 grade point average and was selected as a National Merit Scholar. The other students thought she had it made. They had no idea that this young lady lived in fear. Thoughts of failure haunted her every day. She had created a sand castle of perfection in her mind, but the winds and tides threatened it every minute. She became obsessed with not failing in anything—including the perception of others that she was a relaxed, fun person.

Like the rest of us, teenagers can tell if acceptance is conditional. They want to be loved for who they are, not how they perform. They feel they live on a scale all day every day. They need someone to care about them whether they succeed or fail. That's real love. A young man wrote me:

Rodney,
I really need my parents' love. Yeah, I know they love me, but a lot of the time it seems like all they really care about is grades or

school. All my Dad cares about is the SAT and college. It just seems like good grades and good work is expected out of me. Rewards or praise aren't given, nothing. I just wish he would be proud of me for me . . . not because I got an A in Physics.

My Mom doesn't really pressure me about grades, but she doesn't really have time for me. I know it's not her fault, because she has to work a lot to support me. I only wish we could have some time together. We're so distant right now. Whenever we do get to talk, it's very uncomfortable, because we just don't know each other anymore.

Can you give me any advice? I need it.

Rusty

Some teens use sports as a way to gain some sense of identity, but even then, fitting in with others can be difficult. This young woman wrote about her desire to find a place with her peers.

Dear Rodney,

If my parents, family and anyone else who doesn't know me very well knew how much I really wanted to be someone, they would be shocked. For my whole life I have not been accepted by others. I have always tried to fit in the groups and be someone. Sometimes I get real depressed because I wasn't someone and wasn't accepted. I am a christian, and I believe strongly in Jesus. Therefore when I have a problem or when I get depressed I pray and rely on the Lord. I really want to be somebody, and I really want to fit in, but my interests are completely different than others. I only enjoy one sport and that's swimming. That automatically makes it difficult to fit in a group.

I want to learn how to play other sports, but each time I try I am unsuccessful. I would have to say that one of my many goals in life is to fit in.

Sometimes it is good to be alone, but other times it is best to have a friend to talk to. Friends are a great source when you have a problem and need someone to talk to.

My parents don't know how much I want to have a friend. If they did, it would make them sad.

Sincerely,
Gloria

Many teenagers feel awkward and lonely. Even when parents are a source of strength, the vicious taunts of peers at school can crush a teen's sense of identity.

Dear Rodney,

I don't have any friends. Sometimes I think there's something wrong with me and maybe that's why they don't want to be around me a lot. I cry myself to sleep sometimes. When people make fun of me at school or someplace public, I usually forget about it for the time being and then when I get home, I cry about it privately. My parents realize that I don't have friends, and they are supportive. I wish I knew someone that I could talk to.

Bridgette

But for many adolescents, the home environment is anything but a source of strength. Abuse, addiction, manipulation, confusion, and loneliness are the colors which paint the picture of their lives.

Dear Rodney,

My dad's an alcoholic, and my older brother whose ninteen is an alcoholic, and my younger brother whose thirteen is an alcoholic. I'm fourteen. My dad has kidney stones, and he's in pain a lot of time. He's out of a job right now, and he drinks because of that. He says he's not an alcoholic, and I guess compared to most people he's not.

My little brother is involved with drugs. My mom knows about it, but she won't do anything about it. Too much trouble I guess. I can't go anywhere with my family. I went to the mall with them and my best friend. My older brother drove, and he got stoned in the car. So I stay home all the time.

I'd like to talk to my dad. I'd ask him "why do you do this?" It used to not be this bad, but it has just kept getting worse. And my mom, well, she used to drink, but she doesn't drink much anymore. She lost her job over it some time ago.

I wanted to tell you about me and my old best friend. She's an alcoholic. We went to a party and at the party, one of her fifteen year old friends offered me a drink. I drank it, and I was a little dizzy but my mind was OK. So, I thought another one wouldn't hurt. I don't remember much after that. I remember walking around with a crushed beer can in my hand. I remember my best friend set me up with a girl. On my third drink, everybody started laughing. I was such a fool because I remember hanging over the commode, throwing up, with everyone laughing at me. Later they told me I was praying and asking God for help. That's what they were laughing at.

The next morning I got up and thought—What's the deal with drinking? Are people (like me) stupid or what? But I went to another party, and somebody handed me a beer. I drank it and I thought—This time I'm not going to get sick. I went outside to get my second wind, but all these people were out there smoking pot. Somebody was getting a tattoo. I went back into another room, but everywhere I went, people were getting high. We got home safe, but I don't know how.

The next weekend, I thought—Wow! I don't get it! I know everybody likes to party, but they look so stupid passed out on the floor. My best friend is like that. My Mom won't let me see her anymore. She won't quit drinking. She's been to AA and quit for a year, but then she started again.

Roger

Young people seek peace of heart and peace of mind. Even those who do wild and crazy things are actually trying to find meaning in their lives so they can be at peace. But their search for peace often leads them to despair because they seek it from the wrong sources. Instead of real peace, they experience a false version. I want to use the acrostic PEACE to describe the deceptive and dangerous ways many teenagers seek fulfillment, contentment, and peace. These ways promise hope, but they produce heartache.

P—Pressure

Pressure from peers warps teenagers' perceptions and colors their choices. I've heard the stories about how parents "used to walk ten miles in ten feet of snow to school and work three jobs after school" and of all the other tough things they had to go through when they were young. They compare their teenage years to their children's and say, "My son and my daughter have got it made in the shade! I'd give anything in the world to have had the things my son or daughter have when I was a teenager."

Teenagers may have much more in material terms today, but they also have far more pressure to use drugs, join gangs, and have sex to "find meaning" in life. Cultural pressures on teenagers are enormous. On top of this are the normal pressures in the home. Parents have legitimate expectations for sons and daughters to clean up their rooms, take care of their daily chores, meet their curfew, and make good grades. If they don't live up to those expectations, they feel like a failure. When they go to school, they face even more pressure to make a certain grade. And if they don't pass the class, they are considered a failure. If they try out for the cheerleading squad and they don't make it, or if they try out for the band and they don't make it, or they go out for the football team and they get cut, what do they feel like? They feel like they are failures.

If they have failed at home and at school, where do they go? They go out in the real, cruel world. There is a mentality in our society that whatever it takes, you must succeed. No matter what price you have to pay, you must succeed. We live in a performance-oriented society. If you don't perform, if you don't meet those certain standards, or you don't live up to those expectations, our society pushes you to the side.

The family used to be a safe haven to help us handle the difficulties of life. Today, the family is a major part of the problem for most young people, not a part of the solution. The 50-percent divorce rate in our country forces many young people to choose between living with either their mom or dad. They often have to fit into a new blended family with all of their awkward, strained dynamics. In all kinds of families, kids feel tremendous, overwhelming stress. They want some way out.

E—Escape

In the face of this pressure, young people want to *escape* by giving in to the demands of others or copping out. People who face an enormous amount of pressure automatically try to eliminate the pain and lower the level of pressure. At that point, young people are tremendously vulnerable to deception. Peers, magazines, television, and all other media promise peace and happiness if we will only buy—whatever is for sale at that moment. These things look good. The promises seem real. And often they feel good—for a short time. Then comes emptiness, or worse, destruction.

A—Available

Drugs, sex, gangs, cigarettes, and countless other lures are *available* to help them escape. When we try to find a way of escape, we are exposed to a wide variety of options, even for very young people. I drove past an elementary school recently on my way to a speaking engagement in Ft. Worth. In front of the school, I saw a sign which read: "You are now entering a drug-free zone." I thought to myself, *I doubt that!* Unfortunately, there isn't a community in America which is exempt from drugs. Tomorrow morning you could get in your car and drive to the nearest elementary school, and in less than thirty minutes, you could find just about any kind of illegal drug that you'd want. You could find contacts who would sell you—or your eight-year-old child—virtually any type of illegal drug.

Recent studies depict the traumatic atmosphere of today's teenagers. This is the environment our kids experience.

Every day:
- 1,000 unwed teenage girls become mothers
- 1,106 teenage girls get abortions
- 4,219 teenagers contract sexually transmitted diseases
- 500 teenagers begin using drugs
- 1,000 teenagers begin drinking alcohol
- 135,000 teenagers take guns or other weapons to school
- 3,610 teenagers are assaulted
- 80 teenagers are raped
- 2,200 teenagers drop out of high school
- 6 teenagers commit suicide.[2]

Most parents today pay to provide cable television for their children. Many of the cable channels have explicit and violent shows and movies. Indeed, the average person watches approximately 9,230 sexual scenes, or implied sexual scenes, in the course of one year on television. Of those ten thousand sexual scenes, over 80 percent occur between single people.[3] What does that say to us? It says, "It's okay for young people to have sex outside marriage. You don't have to worry about the consequences." This perspective promises all the pleasure with none of the guilt.

Television has become a staple in our lifestyle, but we don't recognize the consequences of this addiction. The average American family has the TV turned on seven hours a day. After accounting for work, school, sleeping, and eating, the TV absorbs virtually all of the remaining time—time that could be spent in meaningful conversation. And unlike watching television, conversation takes effort. It is much easier to sit, placid and passive, in front of the tube instead of genuinely communicating with each other.

Author and speaker Zig Ziglar observed our culture in his excellent book *Raising Positive Kids in a Negative World:* "Two-bathroom homes eliminated cooperation, television eliminated conversation and the second car eliminated association." These luxuries are ruining our ability to relate to each other. Ziglar wrote specifically about the damaging consequences of being absorbed in television, "The behavior TV causes is bad, but the behavior it prevents is worse. You are what you are and where your are because of what has gone into your mind. You can change what you are and where you are by changing what goes on in your mind."[4] But that takes focused attention, effort, and—a precious commodity in our day—repentance from passive, harmful behavior to positive, relationship-building behavior.

C—Curiosity

Curiosity fuels the desire to experiment and try new behaviors and experiences. The natural and normal desire to experiment and try new things is driven and distorted by emotional pain and peer pressure. For instance, a young woman may have been sexually abused, or she may feel intense guilt for sleeping with her boyfriend. In either case, the internal stresses can tear her apart with anger and shame. But if she takes a hit of crack cocaine, she can eliminate all of her pain and all of her problems for twenty minutes. That doesn't seem very long, does it? But those few minutes may be a delicious escape for one whose life is a living hell. Curiosity is driven by the desire to eliminate the pain and the pressure in young people's lives.

Radio, magazine, and TV ads feed young people's curiosity. These services are designed to produce a sense of desire and a feeling of emptiness if the viewer doesn't have a particular product. And prime-time programming contains all kinds of behaviors which run counter to Christian principles. Premarital sex, cursing, drinking, violence, lying, and a host of other evils are regularly portrayed as acceptable and even desirable. Young people want to know what it feels like to experience these things. And they try them. For example, by the time seniors graduate from high school:

- 93 percent have used alcohol at some time
- 27 percent have used stimulants
- 16 percent have used cocaine
- 15 percent have used hallucinogens[5]

Curiosity is certainly not a negative characteristic. It is neutral. Curiosity is the energy of exploration and experimentation. If it is directed toward good and healthy pursuits, it produces creativity and growth. If, however, naturally curious young people drift toward harmful behaviors, this energy can result in hurt instead of health, and misery instead of growth.

E—Empty

All of these escapes only leave teenagers *empty*: hurting, wanting more, and vulnerable to more pressure to try new things. They have tried everything the world has to offer—alcohol, drugs, sex, you name it. Yet that longing in their hearts remains. Tragically, they find themselves starting all over again, trying to find answers to life's problems, but looking in the wrong places.

Every adolescent goes through bumps and bruises in the awkward teen years, and, surprisingly, most of them make it through okay! The real question is not: *How do we prevent our children from making any mistakes?* The more significant questions are: *How can I help my teenager learn to make good, mature decisions?* and *How can I help my teenager learn from his or her mistakes?* If we try to control their lives too much, we will lose the credibility we can have with them. But if we treat them with honesty and respect, allowing them to be a part of the decision-making process—even for discipline—they will learn and grow.

Don't make too many assumptions about the pressures your teenager faces. Sometimes I hear a parent say things like, "Jim must be doing pretty well. He sure is busy at school and he has a part-time job so he can make some money. He can't get in too much trouble if he's that busy!" Part-time jobs or other activities can be very positive, or they may actually erode a teen's sense of security and strength, as in this teenager's life.

Dear Mom and Dad,

Well here I am. I don't really know what to say. You guys know everything about me. Well, at least you thought you did, but I never told you that my heart is broken because I did not want you guys to have a broken heart too. I never told you or anyone else about why I quit my job one year ago. I quit because there was these three guys who just looked at me as a toy. If I was in the back, somehow they would always find out and go back there and push me against walls, put me in corners. One time it was even the men's bathroom.

Why would someone want to hurt me? I don't do nothing to deserve it. If you knew the pain that I was going through when I was hanging around with the "wrong" crowd! They were always drinking, smoking, smoking pot, but I never once had the urge to do it because if you were with them the whole time, look how they felt in the morning, or how dumb they acted sometimes, picking fights with people. I wish I could tell you how I felt when my brother and his friends would make fun of me because I went to church. I wish you knew how I felt after I stopped coming. I was not the same person.

I am so sorry we get in such big arguments or when I disobey you. I feel like I am a nobody, sometimes I feel as if nobody cares, but sometimes I feel that I don't want to be here. Why can't I be that person? Why does that person have so much and I have none? I feel so pressured to have sex with boys in my school. I love you always. I'm sorry.

Natalie

And divorce devastates kids. Parents are often so focused on their own wounds and heartaches, they can't face the realities of their children's needs. I'm not trying to make divorced people feel guilty. I'm only suggesting that you need to recognize the very real stress divorce creates in each family member's life, and that you should have a plan to relieve some of these stresses.

One young lady was deeply hurt because her father pursued a new life without even bothering to talk to her about it. She may have been his child, but she was a growing, maturing young woman who deserved respect and communication.

Dear Rodney,

When my dad began dating after a long divorce, he hid so much from me. He wouldn't tell me who "she" was or where they went. I felt so unimportant. This lady could turn out to be my step-mother, yet I haven't the slightest idea what she's like. Now I'm dating and my dad expects a boy to call him (though he doesn't live in the same house as me) and ask permission. Biblical, yes, sensible, no. I really wanted to know about his life and he refused to answer any questions. Now he demands to know about mine and I tend to try to keep things equally secret. If he only knew . . . my whole life he has said, "when you're older." Now I feel as a teenager, that hearing his experiences should prepare me for life. No. Everything is confidential.

Dottie

The ultimate goal of adolescence is to find some sense of identity—to be somebody, to get attention for something, to carve out a niche. This is not some passive, expendable aim. It is a consuming drive! But most adolescents want to look cool while they're striving for it. Parents' opinions about them become less significant. Peers' opinions become paramount. Their quest is shaped by a number of factors, including the values of their peer group, their personality, ability, opportunities, and often, the influence of another adult.

The peer group's values are established by the perceived leader and the "consent of the governed." Whatever is considered valuable and is reinforced by praise becomes the societal norm for the group. For instance, one group may value athletic ability.

They form their own clique and allow only those who meet a certain level of athletic prowess to participate. Another group is formed by the kids who are socially "cool." Still another culture is established by those who use drugs and who have their own language, place to hang out, ways to get high, and expectations of secrecy for those within the group. Even Christian kids naturally band together because of their values. Each group has an internal structure (almost never stated) and perceived enemies which serve to force the group to bond in defense.

Personality, ability, and opportunities shape a teen's identity. Athletics, scholastic achievement, appearance, family background, talents, class standing, and a host of other factors combine with the drive (or lack of drive) to achieve to determine the person's level of achievement. This is affected by the available opportunities. An extremely bright person may be held back academically by the values of his peer group. It may not be cool to be smart. Or those gifted in certain areas may not have the opportunities to perform and establish their identity in that area. Usually, however, people find some way to do what they do best. Some of them even create their own opportunities.

A critical factor in giving young people the opportunity to achieve is the affirmation of an adult. This person may be a teacher, coach, Sunday school teacher, counselor, aunt, uncle, grandparent, or anyone else who believes in the teenager when no one else does. Perhaps this adult is a confidant who listens and affirms. Maybe this person pushes the gifted young person to the next level of achievement. Maybe this person is simply there after school with a hug and a kind word. In a thousand different ways, these people play a vital role in shaping the identity of young people by communicating the powerful, life-changing message, "I care about you! I believe in you!"

Every teenager needs at least one person like this. And every parent needs to know that this person is available and active in the teenager's life. When parents and young people can't communicate, this person can be the switchboard which untangles the lines and makes the necessary connections for communication.

Quite often, this person is the most important stepping-stone at this critical time in a young person's life. If your teenager doesn't have somebody, the first thing to do is to ask God to provide, then look for His answer. Sometimes, He provides without us making a move. Other times, all we need to do is to be aware of teachers, coaches, relatives, or others who show a special interest in our children. Then we can tell them how much their friendship means to us and to our child. This gentle nudge may be all that is needed to move the relationship to a deeper, more attentive level.

If no one surfaces to mentor your child, consider talking to a counselor, pastor, or teacher to get some ideas about someone you can ask to take more interest in your teenager. You can't orchestrate a special relationship like this. All you can do is pursue the possibilities with an open mind and open heart and see who God provides. And keep praying!

Reflection/Discussion Questions

1. Who are some people who communicate respect and love to you? How do they do this?
2. What are some strength areas in your life? How do you feel when you "shine" in doing them?
3. How can you communicate love and respect to your teenager?
4. List your teenager's strengths. When was the last time you complimented him or her on these?
5. Look again at the section on pages 45-50 dealing with how teenagers (and adults) seek peace through ways that produce more heartache. What are some ways your teenager experiences:
   - pressure
   - escape
   - availability of drugs, sex, etc.
   - curiosity
   - emptiness
6. Who is a significant adult who can instill confidence and wisdom in your teenager? What steps are appropriate to encourage this relationship? What steps are inappropriate and manipulative?

CHAPTER 5

. . . My Real Desires

Teenagers have deeply held dreams and desires. And they can change in a heartbeat!

Dear Rodney,
I think alot of times my mom might try too hard. Since she is a single mother and my dad's never around, she feels what she does will determine who I am. She wants me to do things sometimes that I don't want. For instance: I'm in scouts, she wants me to get my eagle however that is not something I want to do. I know she had good intentions and reasons why, but I have my own reasons. I think if we could sit down and talk about it, it would help. She doesn't understand that I am not going to be happy accomplishing something that I have no desire to accomplish. She must understand, I am going to be whoever I make myself. If she pushes me to do something that is not my desire, I'll just drop it sooner or later.

Russell

One young woman told me emphatically, "My parents are the *last* people in the world I'd tell my real feelings and desires! They just wouldn't understand, and besides, they'd *kill* me if they knew." The girl may have overstated her parents' reaction a bit, but she made her point. The hormonal changes and new independence of adolescence clash with parents' desires for control. Too many parents remember what they did when they were teenagers, and they somehow want to keep their children from being as stupid! This may be a worthy goal, but the method is suspect.

Instead of drawing the net tightly around the freedom-seeking teenager, parents should enter into dialogue with him. A father may say to his son, "I remember some of the stunts I did when I was your age. Some of them were really fun. Some were insane! Most boys your age feel like they want to conquer the world. They want to try new things." The father can let the son know that it is normal to have those feelings and desires. And as the communication develops, the father can relate some of the consequences of stupid pranks.

Lack of communication isolates parent and child from each other. They then become more rigid and defiant, and communication becomes more difficult. A beautiful fourteen-year-old girl I know told a friend's mother, "I can't talk to my folks about relationships with boys. They don't even know I'm interested in boys! They think I'm still a little kid!" The exasperation came through in her voice. She didn't necessarily want to tell her parents all her secret thoughts and dreams about boys. She just wanted to be respected as a young lady who had normal desires for relationships. Her parents are Christians. They know she's growing up, but they didn't acknowledge her interest in boys quickly enough, so she assumed they were ignorant or disinterested.

They certainly weren't disinterested. They just didn't anticipate the changes so soon! And they learned from their error. They now ask her questions (usually somewhat oblique questions) about boys in her class, and they talk about other girls' relationships with boys. They don't get much information, but the conversations are an adequate basis for the future.

Parents often complain that their children don't tell them about their dreams and desires. The reason the teenagers are silent is that the parents overreact. Parents need to learn to bite their lips when kids have the courage to speak from the heart! Don't instantly condemn or correct. That is a sure way to end the conversation—and never start the next one! And keep your eyeballs in their sockets too. Play it cool. Ask a nonthreatening follow-up question or two, and ask the teenager for his or her own interpretation of the situation. Realize that the adolescent's openness is a clear statement of trust, and don't violate that trust.

Kids want a lot of things. Some are more in touch with their desires than others, but deep down, they all want meaningful relationships. They may say they want a new CD or car or tickets to the concert or something else, but what they really want is love. One youth communicated this to me very clearly.

Dear Rodney,
I really wish my mom and dad would pay attention to me. I grew up very self-conscious because I wasn't sure of who loved me. I grew up with money, so my mom felt, and still feels, that shopping, spending money, etc., can fix all the world's hurts. I became really hard on myself to the point where I got straight A's or else I would just emotionally tear myself up. To this day, I still strive to get A+'s and have a good chance of being in the top three in my class. But that just doesn't seem good enough, I guess.

I also didn't trust people very much, and therefore it was hard to have close friends. As I grew older it seemed the more unhappy I got. I needed something to fill the void and in the beginning I started turning to guys. I did some things that I know did not please God, but at the time this one guy, a senior (I was a freshman) made me feel so special, loved, and wanted, and I wasn't really sure about those feelings, but I liked them. He was a Christian guy, and right when it became where sex was the next logical step, he broke off the relationship. As much as it hurt, I am glad he broke it off because I didn't have the strength to say "No."

I mostly kept my insecurities inside and put on a mask for everyone. They all thought I had it all together. I had expensive clothes and jewelry. I laughed with them and acted as if nothing bothered me. I felt that no one would understand, or better yet, care. Around this time, two people came into my life, a guy and a good friend that I had known for forever. This guy and I had grown up together, but suddenly over one summer, we became close friends. He honestly adored me and would do anything for me. We have dated off and on for the past three years. He has given me some of the best and worst times of my life. But because he cared so much, I stayed with him. I always had fresh roses because he constantly bought me some. He wined and dined me (not literally) and eventually I fell in love. It was different because this relationship didn't seem to violate God. Well, it was too easy, I guess, and we broke it off for good, but we stayed friends. Well, it was a unique friendship because we used each other for, I guess, pleasure. It made both of us feel icky because it seemed wrong, but once again, it filled my empty void.

Well, needless to say, it didn't work out and I don't know if this guy and I even have a friendship left.

Sarah became my best friend our junior year. Everyone expected to see us together. She seemed like the perfect person to help me fix my problem, but I couldn't tell her. She made me feel secure, but a lot of times she just didn't pay attention. I figure that's a lot to do with that she doesn't know. I figure that until I tell her there may be a wall there. She has made me feel special, though, and has probably helped the most. I still don't feel close to my parents.

Can you give me any advice which would help me?

Your friend,
Lori

Adolescence is a time to dream and cultivate a sense of purpose in life. Some teenagers have a great desire to help others. Learn to appreciate their hearts—even if they want to do something that could be dangerous. We may hope they will choose vocations which are safe and secure, but we can affirm their desire to serve.

Dear Rodney,
I have a cousin who is a policeman in North Carolina, and ever

since I can remember, I have watched "Hill Street Blues," "True Blue," and "Rescue 911." I have always been interested in our law enforcement system and how so many crooked cops could keep from getting caught. This system needs a lot of help.

There is another reason I want to be in law enforcement. I want to reach kids who need help. I am shy and have a hard time speaking in front of other people, but I still want to help them. I want to tell them somebody cares enough to protect them and help them live a better life.

Too bad my parents don't see it like this. They think I'm asking for some deranged gunman to come and kill me. So I don't discuss it with them. But this is what I feel like I need to do. To lay my life on the line and show people that someone cares enough to lay their life on the line for them, a total stranger committed to help stop crime.

I wish my parents could understand that they can't keep me sheltered for the rest of my life. I have got to get out because I am being suffocated completely and totally. I am going to flip my lid soon. They want me to go to college which I have no problems with, but they clam up when it comes to the Police Academy. They don't want to think about their only daughter going and becoming a cop. I thought they wanted me to pick my own career, and when I do, they hate it. They keep saying it's just a phase I'm going through and it will pass. Yeah, right. It won't stop that easily. I think this is what God wants me to do, so I'd better do it.

Stacy

The quest for independence spurs many teenagers to pursue interests very different from their parents' desires. Some teens say they are interested in unusual vocations or activities just to get a reaction from their parents. These fads will pass. But some genuinely want to follow a different drummer. It is a wise parent who can tell the difference—or who has enough patience to wait and let the teenager change his mind (ten or twelve times!). It is perfectly understandable for parents to express their dreams for their children's futures, but be careful not to devalue the young person's own sense of destiny and purpose.

Dear Rodney,
Mother and Dad probably wouldn't like it. I've just started college and I've changed majors from engineering to architecture and business to something else pretty soon I'm sure. While I can do these things, they don't interest me at all. The things I really love are music (I play piano) and film. I'm taking one video/film class right now and I love it, but my parents want me to study something that I'll be able to support a family with (and move out soon). They would never let me just study piano, even if I could afford to pay for it myself. I don't know what I'll do. The indecision really sucks.

Debbie

But this teenager had the opposite problem. His parents wanted him to pursue a career in music.

Dear Rodney,
My problem is everybody in my family has a talent in music and they know something about it. They say that I can apply music to my life, and use it in many ways. I think that if I could tell them in some way that I hate music, they might leave me alone about it. They will probably give me no choice in it what so ever. My real interests are sports. Basketball and Baseball mainly. I played them ever since I was in second grade. So they are my real interests. My problem with music is I'm no good at it. Like memorizing the notes and so on. For example at church there is a group called bells that my mom helps direct. She gives me no choice and makes me play. After one year of it I don't like it and find out I'm no good at it. She makes me go do it this year too. If there was only a way I could tell them my real desires. This is my problem, and I hope I'll find a solution, but if I don't I have god to rely on.

Stephen

Adolescent desires are shaped by hormones, but our culture adds a powerful and deceptive dimension to the lure of money, sex, power, status, affection, and pleasure: We think we *deserve* all of these things. Every day, kids hear of athletes signing a twenty or even fifty million dollar contract. They read of people hitting the jackpot in the lottery and getting rich overnight. They see television shows of young, attractive people having sex without ever experiencing pregnancy, disease, guilt, or the responsibility of providing for the child. And they see thousands of beer commercials with young, strong, tan, happy people drinking their favorite brew. Our kids don't think about alcohol-related traffic deaths, broken families, and ruined lives. They want something for nothing. They want it *all* for nothing.

People are mesmerized by beer commercials on television. I like to watch sports on the tube, and a lot of the advertisers are beer companies. Their ads are incredibly attractive. They paint very glamorous pictures. Take the one which has Steve Winwood jamming in the background of a bar scene. In walks a "hot chick": long blonde hair, tight leather skirt, fishnet hose, gorgeous figure. All of the guys in the bar are foaming at the mouth! Every step she takes is right to the beat of the music. All of a sudden, a guy who looks like he just stepped off a *GQ* cover comes into the picture. He gives her the "look" as they enjoy a cold brew together. In only a few seconds, we see the two of them leaving the bar arm in arm.

And the commercial ends and we go back to sportscasters Frank, Al, and Dan. But the image and the suggestions aroused by the commercial don't end. It only takes an IQ slightly above plant life to figure out where this couple is going. But is good, guilt-free sex always the result of downing a few brews? Hardly. Sure, alcohol usually does loosen people up. They become less inhibited, and they may laugh a little more easily. But the hard facts about the effects of alcohol are somewhat less glamorous. The cameras don't show the marriages devastated because a spouse came in loaded and screamed at everybody, blew the family budget, or said something embarrassing in front of others. The cameras don't reflect the statistics showing the correlation between alcohol and spousal and child abuse, violent crimes, health problems, and divorce. The cameras don't show teenagers, junior high kids, and even younger kids who start down the path of alcohol and drug use because it looks so attractive on the screen. The cameras don't show pictures of bodies mangled in alcohol-related car accidents, which account for almost half of the injuries and deaths in accidents each year. The cameras don't show the hurt, anger, loneliness, and heartache of families ripped apart as a result of alcohol. Would people affected in these ways say, "You know, it just doesn't get any better than this!"?

Many families prime their children to be observant and analytical by asking them, "What is the real message of this commercial?" or "What does this commercial say that beer drinking will do for you?" or "What are some differences between the message of this commercial and the truth?" Television is a passive medium. People become zombies when they watch it. They typically turn off their analytical processes and simply absorb the messages. Questions like these will help your family accurately interpret the messages they see on television, and then even these deceptive messages can be used to strengthen their values.

The unrealistic expectations kids can receive from TV warp their perceptions. They expect more and are bitterly disappointed when they don't get it. So they use the things they see—drugs, sex, food, sports, and people—to fill the hole in their lives. The consequences just make the hole bigger and deeper. And the cycle continues.

At the center of it all, what teenagers (and the rest of us too) really desire is to love and be loved. We cherish relationships. We long for meaningful interaction with friends and family. This young lady said it well.

Dear Rodney,
Many things have deeply upset me. It's so hard to try and please everyone . . . my family, my friends, my boyfriend. I try so hard and yet sometimes I fail. There have been times when I've given up and given in to peer pressures like cussing and drinking. I want to make my parents proud by making good grades. I want to make my friends happy by being there for them and just being a friend. I want to make my boyfriend happy by being the Christian girlfriend he wants and needs. I want to make God happy by being the Christian He wants me to be!
All of these things I want, I feel like I can't accomplish them to the fullest. Because of that I get down on myself and become so angry with myself I may take it out on others and do just the

opposite of what I wanted to do. I hope you can understand how I want these things so bad yet I cannot accomplish them. Please understand! Try!

Lisa

Reflection/Discussion Questions

1. What were your dreams when you were young?
2. How can you tell what your teenager's dreams really are?
3. What are your goals and expectations for your teenager? Are they appropriate? Why or why not?
4. Is it hard for you to "let your teenager fly"? Explain.
5. How can legitimate concern about your teenager's dreams be communicated in positive, encouraging ways?
6. How do you feel when a dream dies? How can you be a "dream encourager" to your teenager?

CHAPTER 6

. . . Why I'm So Angry!

I can see it in their eyes. They are full of fury. Perhaps it's their developmental phase. Perhaps it's the culture we live in. Perhaps they feel insecure because of a breakdown in their family. Whatever the cause, teenagers express their anger to me with an intensity that is sometimes shocking. Here are a few examples of their wrath.

Dear Mom and Dad,

I wish you only knew how angry I used to be. I have gone through a lot these past two years since the separation. I just want to tell you my anger Mom. I know what you have done. Jenny, your best friend, told me about the drugs. The same cocaine, marijuana, and crack you told me to stay away from you don't. Alcoholism is another problem Mom. I don't even try alcohol because I have 50 percent chance at being an alcoholic. (I don't want to try alcohol though. It is a sin.)

Why did you make me baby-sit till 4:30 during a school year on a week night at the most emotionally unstable part of my life? I know about your adultery, Mom. One more thing you had me stay away from! How do I know? Three ways— 1—Jenny told me;

2—Jim's friend told me, and 3—I found a box for contraceptive sponges in the garbage can during the separation. I had seen it in a grocery bag earlier that week. I know that my step father's a drug dealer, Mom.

Dad, I was angry at you also. I didn't like Mary, my former step-mother, because I felt it was too soon after the divorce to find another wife. I just know it wouldn't last, Dad. I hated you for moving her in in June of last year while I was at Youth Camp, especially after I got saved that week and gave myself to Christ. Our home felt sinful.

I moved in with Dad for reasons I never told anyone. I feared for my life. I was afraid one of Mom's slimy boyfriends would take my virginity by force. I felt I'd get caught up in drugs and alcohol. I don't visit you, Mom because I don't like your morals. You also treat me like I'm five and want me to act thirty-five while you act like you're twenty-five. Let me be fifteen and a half, Mom.

Dad, I was angry for you making me do all the chores. I mother my siblings, Dad. I'm the Christian head of house. Mom, I don't think you love me. I have never got any money from you to buy my needs: (Clothes, shoes, Band Camp . . .).

Both of you have emotionally and mentally abused me. I prayed for God to help me forgive you. I love and care about you both. I want you to know that I love you and forgive you. I want you both to know I love you and will always be your oldest daughter.

Melynda

Dear Mom and Stanley,

I want to be completely honest with you. My life has been a mess in my eyes. And I have to say some of it, I think, is your fault. You know Mom I lost my daddy. I was only six. But I never had real sympathy. I put up walls in my life. I never wanted to be close to someone. I was so afraid they would leave me also. Then you married Stanley. I was and have been very bitter toward Stan. He wanted to love me, and I brushed him away, thinking no one could take my daddy's place. I put up a fake image. No one, No one knew what was going on in my life. I was really closed up, locked up tight so nobody could hurt me again.

I feel really confused. I want to be close to you and Stanley, but I'm really mad at both of you. I want to be close to my real dad, but I'm mad at him because he's not here. I want to run and hide from all this. And I guess that's what I've done, but it doesn't make me happier.

Now I don't know how to be close. I feel like I've got a door on my heart that is locked up. I keep every body from hurting me—or I thought I did, but I also keep people out. I blame you, Mom, for breaking up with dad. I blame dad for leaving, I blame Stanley even though he has really tried to be nice to me. I guess I blame him for trying to take my daddy's place. And I blame me for locking the door. I want out.

Rich

Dear Rodney,
I grew up with alcoholics—my father and my brother, and I hate them! I hate them! I know that's not right either. I'm not supposed to hate them, but I don't know how to deal with it. I can't talk to my mom about them. She gets real upset when I try to talk to her and says they're doing the best they know how. They can't help it. My mom said my dad doesn't know how to love.
I don't go to drinking parties. I was raised around drinking and I don't want any part of it. I wish my dad and my brother would go away. Or die or something. I can't wait until I can leave home. I don't want to be in a family like this any more.
Can you help me?

Philip

Teenagers have a strong sense of justice. When they believe they have been violated, they react strongly. Many of the kids who talk to me describe their anger over partiality in the home. They feel that a brother or sister is the parents' favorite. And they are mad about it.

Rodney,
I am angry because I am the only girl and I get treated so unfairly. I have three brothers and they just sit on their butts and do nothing. I clean, cook, and take care of things. My brothers

are always getting me in trouble. They rag on me all the time and when I tell my parents they don't care so I take care of it myself and then I get in trouble.

I wish you would come kick them!

Trish

Dear Mom and Dad,
I'm angry at you for many reasons. First of all, I feel that I'm silent because no one hears or pays attention to me. I feel like I get blamed for anything that happens, it's never my brother's fault. I'm really mad at the fact that you'll act like your marriage is perfect and its not.

Get real, and get a life!

Nina

Dear Rodney,
I'm so angry at my parents! I'm angry because my mother always pays attention to my sister. I guess she has to since she's always getting in trouble. For the past four years our life has revolved around my sister, and my sister only. It seems like they never pay attention to me. I guess that's why I'm so angry.

Leslie

Adolescence is a whirlwind. Changes occur at a dizzying pace. Teenagers desperately need stability, but they are in the process of becoming independent, so their primary source of stability—the home—is often seen as a threat instead of a refuge. Every day at school or in the neighborhood, kids ridicule each other, laugh at each other, and ignore each other. Sometimes they beat the tar out of each other! They feel alone. They feel hurt. They feel angry.

Teenagers from strong, Christian families experience their share of anger in this threatening environment, but imagine the level of intense bitterness in the lives of those who don't have emotional resources. Every night on the news we see this rage in action. A young man robs a store and shoots a female clerk in the chest with a double-barreled shotgun. When the police search his home, they find rap songs espousing violent hatred for women and police. A group of young men rape and murder two fifteen-year-olds "for the fun of it." Gang violence and drugs are the nightly fare of the local newscasts. In fact, these acts of brutality, hopelessness, and greed are now so common we aren't shocked any more. This behavior has become normal in our culture.

"But my kid isn't doing this kind of thing!" you insist. And you may be right. But all our children are exposed to the the escalating levels of violence, drugs, gangs, guns, racial hatred, and a hundred other forms of injustice. Our kids may not be actively participating, but they experience the fear of becoming victims.

For many teenagers, the incidents of today are complicated by the wounds of yesterday. The unresolved hurts from abuse or abandonment leave them thin-skinned and vulnerable to the slightest wrong or perceived wrong. They are powder kegs with exposed fuses looking for a match, and the matches are all around them. One teenager expressed her fury toward her parents.

Dear Rodney,
If my parents knew how I felt about them, I probably wouldn't live here. I hate my parents! I like living as a christian and they put me down. They call me "stupid" and my dad calls me "a bitch." I hate living in my house, and I wish they would die. My parents are cruel and totally put me down, all the time. The only family I can trust is my friends.

Deborah

When the fuse is lit and the powder keg explodes, the angry teenager often follows the example of a parent. If a dad yells and curses, a son probably will too. If a mother sulks and withdraws, the daughter will follow that model. Adolescents don't sit down and decide how to act when they are angry. They do what they have seen.

Most Christians don't know how to handle anger—theirs or anyone else's. They believe righteous indignation is an allowed response to murder, rape, and abortion, but angry reactions to anything else is sinful. Certainly, most expressions of anger are sinful, but the emotion of anger is not sin. Anger is a response to injustice (or perceived injustice), and injustice takes many forms: a friend who ignores, a teacher who arbitrarily changes a grade, a coach who picks someone else to start even though we've worked harder, a girlfriend who dumps us, a parent who won't listen and harshly punishes or avoids us . . . the list goes on and on. The apostle Paul instructed the believers in Ephesus, "Be angry, and do not sin" (Eph. 4:26). That is, acknowledge the feeling of anger, but learn to express it appropriately, not in violence or revenge.

Most parents feel very uncomfortable with their children's expressions of anger, and respond verbally or nonverbally, "You shouldn't be angry!" This is the wrong message. The fact is, people feel angry because they feel they are the victim of an injustice. Telling people who feel like victims not to feel angry makes them feel victimized again. They experience another injustice, and their anger builds.

Anger is usually the surface emotion. Under it lies hurt or fear. Some have been deeply hurt. They don't want to hurt again. They are afraid of experiencing rejection, failure, abandonment, punishment, or the unknown. Anger seems safer to communicate than more vulnerable emotions, especially for males, so they hide their hurt under a veil.

Perhaps if we could look deep into an angry person and see the hurt and fear, we would be more patient with them. Maybe we would comfort them. But most parents feel very threatened by their children's expressions of anger. An adolescent's outbursts, withdrawal, or passive-aggressive sarcasm make some feel like failures as parents. It makes some feel out of control. It makes many want to clamp down on the teenager, which only makes the problem worse.

Encourage your teenager to be honest about his anger, and assure him you won't tell him he's stupid for feeling that way. But also give him guidelines about appropriate expressions of his anger. For example, you can say, "I want you to be honest with me about how you feel. I promise not to interrupt or correct you while you're talking, except maybe to ask you to explain something. And I want us to have guidelines: No yelling, no cursing, and no blaming. Will you agree to give it a try under those conditions for each of us?"

You may not like what you hear when you invite your teenager to be honest about his or her anger. It may be explosive. It may be totally irrational and have very little connection with the truth as you perceive it. But remember, the first goal is to begin to communicate, not to solve all the problems. A good way to end the first (or the first few) honest conversations is to say, "I think I understand what you're saying. Let me try to say it back to you." When you repeat your teenager's points, don't try to interpret at all. Don't editorialize. Don't demand change. Just relate them as clearly as possible, including his own observations and his feelings.

Then say, "Is that what you said? Did I miss anything?" You probably did! Patiently listen to his corrections and additions, and you will be on your way to establishing trust in the relationship.

Reflection/Discussion Questions

1. How do you express (or repress) your anger?
   ___ verbally
   ___ physically
   ___ emotionally
2. How does your teenager express (or repress) his or her anger?
3. How would your teenager complete this statement:

   The things that make me most angry are . . .

4. How does your family resolve conflict and anger?
5. How do you respond when your teenager is angry? How does your teenager react to you then? Is there a recognizable pattern in this? If so, describe it.
6. What are some positive, constructive ways you can respond to your teenager's anger?
7. What resources do you need to enable you to respond to your teenager's anger more appropriately?

CHAPTER 7

. . . About My Sexuality

Many parents don't want to believe that their little princess or baby boy is thinking about hitting the sheets with someone. They don't think that letting their children watch PG-13 movies and listen to suggestive lyrics will make an impact on them. They can hardly believe that the statistics about "kids having kids" can be true, and if it is, "it's those other people's kids." We live in a highly sexualized society, and the sexualization of children is one of the most glaring problems. On many prime time sitcoms, the jokes revolve around young children talking about sex. The message isn't lost on those who watch.

A young woman wrote about being molested by her father, and also, her sexualized environment.

Dear Rodney,
I have had so many trials in my life concerning sexual activity.
As a child younger than the age of four, I was sexually molested
by my father. I had forgotten about this until just recently. I
talked to my mom about it, and she said she knew, but by the
time she found out it was too late. You see, my dad died when I
was four, so there was nothing she could do about it. She said,

she found out when she was talking to me about little boys. I asked her if all boys looked the same. She asked why, and I told her because I've seen my daddy's. This upset her so she talked to my dad's previous wife. She said that my step brother had said something similar to her. I have held this in for so many years. I only wish my dad knew how much he hurt me.

One Sunday morning about two weeks ago. I had rode home with two guys, Scott and Ben. They took me home and Ben asked me if I wanted to go eat. I asked my mom and she said, "yes." We went to Wendy's, and got the food to go. We rode around for a while. During this time the guys were talking pretty nasty and told me they thought of me as one of the guys. I thought that was pretty good.

As the ride progressed they started talking about their "dawgs" [penises]. So Scott said, "you don't know what a dawg is." I said, "yes I do." Scott said, "Do you want to see one?" I said, "No that's okay." Well, later me and Ben got in an argument and he told me to get out of the car. I wouldn't, so Ben jumped out and tried to pull me out. I started screaming rape, so he jumped in the backseat of the van. I should have known something was up then. He then said, " Are you sure you don't want to see it?" I said, "yeah, I'm sure." The next thing I know he was unzipping his pants. Then he grabbed my arm and pulled it over the seat. The next thing I knew was that I was touching something I shouldn't be.

I started screaming and I finally got away, but he grabbed me again. I finally begged him to let me go. After this happened I told some of my friends what I thought were my friends about it, and one of them told some people. A few days later there were rumors about it, only they weren't the truth. I wanted to tell my mom how this made me feel and about what happened, but I knew I would get in more trouble than I was.

This next thing isn't as bad, but it happened all the same. I was in church one Sunday morning and me and Ben were passing a note. He asked me if I would have sex with him if the time was right. I told him it would depend on what time it was. If we were dating and I knew you loved me then maybe, but if you just come over one day and said "Hey, lets have sex" I would have to say "no." Then he asked about other sexual stuff. I told him it would be under the conditions. Then he asked about kissing. I wouldn't have minded these questions if I thought he cared about me at all. I told a friend about this and she told me to write him a note and tell him how I really feel. I did this, but he never wrote me back. I believe this could have been so much easier if I could have talked to my parents.

Rodney, I'm praying for girls who have been through times like I have. I hope they don't ever let a guy do these things to them. I believe in the long run this has caused me a lot of stress. And I beg them: Please don't be like me and take it and not say anything. If I had it to do over again, I wouldn't have gotten in that bed, or that van or even wrote that note. I think about these things everyday— wondering how my life might have been different if these things never happened. If girls have been through these things, I hope they tell someone. Tell their parents, preacher, teacher or even a friend. But most importantly tell God. He will be their number one fan and supporter through whatever life throws at them.

Millie

Stories and statistics of the sexualization of our young people are alarming.

- 40 percent of ninth graders reported in a 1992 study by The Center for Disease Control that they have already had intercourse.
- Teenagers have more than 400,000 abortions per year, the highest rate for any segment of the population.
- In a 1993 study of high school students by the American Association of University women, 85 percent of girls and 75 percent of boys said they had been the victims of sexual harassment in school.
- Several reports reveal boys clubs in which participants compete with each other for points, some giving different numbers of points for touching particular female body parts,

others simply adding the number of partners for intercourse. One club's leader claimed sixty-three points.

- Explicit, intrusive sexual comments abound in schools. Notes or verbal offers or commands for sex are common even among elementary school grades.
- In a Rhode Island survey, 65 percent of boys and 49 percent of girls said it was "acceptable for a man to force sex on a woman" if they had been dating for six months or more.[1]

Josh McDowell alerted parents to the modern issues of teenage sexuality in his outstanding book *Why Wait?* He lists many pressures on teens and solutions to this all-pervasive problem. In my talks with thousands of young people, I have noticed several important factors which contribute significantly to teenage sexuality. These include:

Curiosity

After watching thousands of sexual scenes on television, thousands of suggestive commercials, and thousands of songs describing the joys of sex, it is no wonder that adolescents want to know, "Is sex as great as they say it is?" The normal adolescent desire to experiment combines with hormonal urges and curiosity. When a boyfriend or girlfriend is willing, the drive is tremendously strong.

Thrills

The excitement of the chase, the exhilaration of doing something new and taboo, and the anticipation of physical release make sex enticing to adolescents.

Desire for Intimacy

All of us need to feel close to someone. For those who feel disconnected, sex is a way of having a sense of intimacy and security. Touch is powerful, and those who desperately want to be loved can mistake sexual touch for real love. They are deeply disappointed when their lover dumps them for someone else. That kind of love is cheap.

Sexual activity is often only one piece of the puzzle. Hurt, anger, broken relationships, and a craving for affection create a tremendously strong drive for sexual encounters, especially among young women. And many boys are only too happy to meet the physical need. The promise of intimacy is shattered, however, resulting in even more hurt and guilt.

One young woman described the complexities of her drive for intimacy and her guilt.

Dear Rodney,

I really don't know where to start. I was given up at birth by my mother and luckily got adopted when I was four months old. As far back as I can remember I've known of my adoption. The two parents I have now have made me feel so lucky. At least until I found out my adoption mother was pregnant with my soon to be sister. I developed a strong hatred towards her. I lost all my sense of morality. All I thought about from the time I was six years old until I was thirteen years old was how I could get rid of her. She took over my family, or at least that was my thought of the matter.

When I was seven I had developed a strong jealousy towards my sister. My jealousy turned into hatred. I slammed my sister's head into the corner of our living room brick fireplace. I split her head wide open. The worst part about it is the fact that instead of hurting from it, I laughed. Over the years my sister and I grew apart. We just seemed to stay at each others throats, and being the oldest, every time I wound up hurting her. I can't believe that I actually became happy seeing her hurt because I got all the attention from my parents. I, in the real sense of the word, became crazy.

People constantly criticized me and mocked me. I found myself hiding in constant pain. I got to the point of being so tired from all the pain I was causing and receiving. I tried suicide six times. I tried to stab my hand and to this day I have a two inch scar where the doctors sewed it up. I slit my wrist, but I got to the doctor's just in time that they stopped the bleeding. I over-dosed on anything from Nyquil to my grandfather's heart medicine. I had my stomach pumped three times. I tried to shoot myself in the head, but knowing nothing about guns, didn't know how to cock it. The last thing I tried was to jump off a four story building, but looking down, it became impossible.

I am thankful that I never succeeded to this day. My parents began to take notice of my actions. My grades in school went from B's to low F's. My mother had taken the time to talk to me, but I told her as well as my father that they were not my real parents and our family sucked. That was the first time I ever saw my father cry. I never understood.

I started stealing money for cigarettes and things I wanted in stores. My mom caught me one day and called a hospital. They suggested counseling. The very first appointment, I was told I needed to be an in patient. The day I went home from the hospital was the day of my new beginning. I now realized just how good I had it. My family was heaven.

As time went by, I started straying away again. I became the age of being able to date. I experimented with drugs to please different guys. I had to quit because the cocaine was killing me. I went through withdrawal for six months. My family never knew simply because I never talked. I was never around. This past year I became sexually involved with my boyfriend. I thought he loved me. I only wanted to please him, so for about five weeks in a row, I slept with him at least five times a weekend. It took me a month to realize he didn't care. I found out the hard way because when I finally stood up and said "no," all he could say was, "Baby, I thought you loved me." I told him if he truly loved me, he would care. He had a sweet remark, but that remark make me realize I as only a toy. I broke up with him the following day.

One month ago I was raped. I lost all my sense of respect. The guy that raped me was twenty-six years of age. He hurt me mentally as well as physically. Physically, he ripped me and bruised my nipples. Mentally, he took away all respect towards myself. I'll never understand why he could do all of that perversion to me and think it was fun. I hate him.

Through my life's struggles, I found myself hating God. I lost my close grandfather. He had Altzheimers and had to be put into a nursing home. A month after being placed in the nursing home, he was diagnosed having pneumonia. He died a week later. The same year my other grandfather fell off a two story building. It split his head wide open. Through a miracle, my grandfather survived. Today he has the mind of an eight year old child. I just don't understand how or why God could do this to me. It's as if I couldn't get hurt anymore. I wish that I could have become closer to my family than I am because to this day my parents still don't know. I wish I could have parents who could put themselves into my shoes and just see what I've gone through.

Gina

And sometimes teenagers pursue sexual relationships out of a desire for safety than for intimacy. One young woman wrote to me of this desire.

Rodney,
My parents would freak out if they knew what I think about them. My parents are not the best, but my Mom tries. My dad could use some help and some prayers. If they knew how I feel they would disown me. They would because my dad don't do his job and it is really tough on me because sometimes me and my boyfriend have fights and sometimes with my mom, and I feel like I am worthless, or like I am being used.
I would love to change my family in the right direction it would be much better, but you can't do that. Sometimes I feel like living with my boyfriend or a very close friend of mine.

Maria

Peer Pressure

"Everybody's doing it!" is a cliche which is too often true. Acceptance by a peer group is one of the strongest needs in a teenager's life, so teens are terribly vulnerable to peer pressure. Sex is a way of gaining popularity with certain people, and through them, the larger group. Girls then feel desirable. Boys feel macho. Both feelings are powerful impulses for teenagers.

Of course, the pressure from a boyfriend or girlfriend can be personal and intense. The standard line, "If you love me you'll let me," is stated in a hundred different ways, but always with the same intent: to use the other person's desire to be accepted as a tool.

Lack of Information

Today's adolescents know more than their parents' generation, but many have misconceptions about sex. Perhaps it is powerful urges clouding the brain's retention of knowledge, but many teenagers believe that a girl can only get pregnant at a certain time during her period, and sex can be unprotected any other time. And though condom use is touted as adequate prevention for HIV, clinical studies show that condoms fail to block the transfer of the HIV virus 31 percent of the time.[2] That's like pointing a six-shooter at your head with two bullets in the chambers and playing Russian roulette. Not very good odds!

Media Pressure

We've already covered this problem sufficiently, but consider the the *sophistication* of the medium of erotic, suggestive material on television and the *quantity of time* spent watching it. Then consider the quantity and the sophistication your teenager sees in the message of living righteously for Christ. Which is greater? Simple math. No contest.

Alcohol and Drugs

People do things when they are high that they wouldn't do if they were thinking clearly. The use of alcohol and other drugs plays an important role in lowering the defenses and stimulating sexual advances.

Early Dating

Studies report that the earlier a person begins dating, the more likely he or she will engage in premarital sex. These studies focused on high school adolescents, but with the sexualization of children, even elementary school children are "practicing" dating. Some think this is cute. I think it is extremely dangerous.

Adolescent girls typically mature faster than boys. One of the consequences of this is that some of them are attracted to older, more physically and emotionally mature boys. When you add to this the deep emotional need young girls have to feel close to someone, it can produce a tempting and destructive dynamic.

One girl wrote:

> Dear Rodney,
> I wish my parents had a clue how I feel about relationships and intimate sex. I wish they knew I just want to get some kind of attention from them. That is why I date older guys and hangout with older friends—it makes me feel like somebody.
>
> Ann

The Law of Diminishing Returns

"I never meant to go this far. It just happened!" To this high school girl, the progression from holding hands to sex seemed to just happen, but the process was thoroughly predictable. Each step in the process is exciting—for a little while. Then the pleasure and thrill subside, and the couple takes the next step to get those feelings again. And they get them! But only for a while, then they have to take another step, and another. Sexual stimulation was meant for the covenant relationship of marriage. It takes tremendous self-control to stop somewhere on the path to intercourse. Or it takes the wisdom to avoid taking the first step.

The media push to sexualize children and their own hormonal urges can be curtailed by helping kids become convinced of the physical, emotional, and spiritual consequences of sexual activity. The apostle Paul wrote to the Galatian believers, "Do not be deceived, God is not mocked; for whatever a man sows, that will he reap also" (Gal. 6:7). The law of the harvest means that we necessarily experience the natural consequences of our actions: We reap *what* we sow; we reap *after* we sow; and we reap *more than* we sow.

Pregnancy, disease, and the possibility of infertility are some possible consequences of promiscuity. Every thirty seconds, a teenager becomes pregnant. The age of these pregnant children is becoming increasingly young. Hundreds of thousands of these pregnancies end in abortion. Sexually transmitted diseases (STDs) are epidemic in our society. Only a generation ago, the two commonly known sexually transmitted diseases, gonorrhea and syphilis, could be treated with penicillin. Today we have twenty common STDs, and the infection rate is so high that it is estimated at least 50 percent of Americans will get STDs by the time they are thirty years old.[3]

The absence of positive role models and the presence of sexual images and other messages has created role confusion in some teenagers. The hormonal urges are not channeled along normal heterosexual paths. One confused adolescent wrote me:

Dear Rodney,

My relationship with my mom has turned into a "You hurt me so I'll hurt you" kind of a deal. My Father lives in Rhode Island. (they're divorced) I have four half sisters (all together) and two half brothers—mom's on her fifth marriage right now. We move around a lot and I get thrown around in the hustle. My stepfather, well, it's kind of like he's not there unless he's yelling at me. My mom says "you need a psychiatrist." She's right, I do. I feel sometimes like no one in the whole world loves me and that anyone who acts like they do are just using me or plotting against me.

I've already had premarridal sex one time. (I was drunk and stoned but I feel its just as much my fault—it is.) So I can't be virgin pure, but I can try to substain from sex until marriage. I've had my fair share of troubles I guess more than the average fifteen year old. I fell into a crowd where every weekend we went out and got drunk or high. It took my getting arrested before I finally realized what was going on.

I fight with Bisexuall feelings day and night. I've told my mom that I like girls and she went histerical and told all her friends how evil I am. That's also one reason she kicked me out of the house.

I really need to gain my morals back as they were when I was very young because I don't seem to have any lately. My friend/x-boyfriend and I are fooling around behind his girlfriend's back and had planned to have sex, but hopefully I can have the courage to tell him I can't anymore and why.

The reason I say I have a real problem with lust is because I can't seem to meet a cute guy w/out picturing him having sex with me. I know teenage girls have "fantasies" but I have sick fantasies of me, another girl, and a guy; torture items (sado-mashicism—however you spell it) and things sort of extra-ordinary.

I get horney if I listen to a certain song, see a certain person, or hear a certain word!

At night I think up pornographic ways to have sex and some-times—(you know).

I've cried a lot lately. I know my mom tries to love me, but she doesn't show it very well. My real father hasn't paid child support in two years and I hear from him once a month.

I really need help.

Eileen

AIDS has received the most attention because of its lethality and because the gay community has focused attention on this disease, but many other diseases ravage young people.

- One third of sexually active young women are infected with chlamydia and/or HPV (human papilloma virus).
- Chlamydia can cause pelvic inflammatory disease (PID). The first infection produces a 25 percent chance of infertility; a second infection produces a 50 percent chance.
- HPV causes at least 90 percent of cervical cancer in women.
- Teenagers are possibly ten times more likely to become infected with STDs than adults because their bodies are relatively immature and more susceptible to disease.[4]

The guilt, shame, hurt, and anger produced by sexual

promiscuity cause devastating emotional consequences. One young lady wrote to Ann Landers:

Dear Ann Landers,
I am sixteen, a junior in high school, and like most of the girls here, I have already lost my virginity. In all the years I've been reading your column, I've never seen the honest-to-goodness truth about this, and I think it's time somebody spoke out.
Take my word for it, girls: sex does not live up to the glowing reports and the hype you see in the movies.
I truly regret that my first time was with a guy I didn't care much about. I'd like to end this relationship and date others, but after being so intimate, it's awfully tough.
Since that first night, he expects sex on every date. When I don't feel like it, we end up in an argument. It's like I owe it to him. I don't think this guy is in love with me, at least he's never said so. I know deep down I am not in love with him either, and this makes me feel sort of cheap.
I realize now that this is a very big step in a girl's life. After you've done it, things are never the same.
My advice is, don't be in such a rush. It's a headache and a worry. (Could I be pregnant?) Sex is not for entertainment. It should be a commitment. Be smart and save yourself for someone you wouldn't mind spending the rest of your life with.
Sign me—Sorry I Didn't and Wish I Could Take It Back [5]

Young men can also experience pangs of guilt. After I spoke at a church a few months ago, a big, handsome young man asked to see me. He sat in the pew in front of me and looked away as he began, "Rodney, I stole something from my girlfriend."

"What was it?" I asked.

"I'm no longer dating her. She's my ex-girlfriend now, but I stole something that I will never be able to give back to her." He paused, then said heavily, "I stole her virginity, and every day I live with the guilt. I knew what we were doing was wrong. Do you think God can forgive me?"

The physical and emotional reasons for being sexually pure are based on common sense. They are reasonable for believers and unbelievers alike. But Christians also have spiritual motivations. The Scriptures command us to be sexually pure, to be faithful to spouses, and to avoid opportunities and even the appearance of sin (Gal. 5:19; 1 Cor. 5:1; 2 Cor. 12:21; Eph. 5:3; 1 Thess. 4:3-4; Heb. 13:4). Self-control in the sexual area of life is a part of our obedience to the lordship of Christ. To the Corinthians, Paul wrote:

> Flee sexual immorality. Every sin that a man does is outside the body, but he who commits sexual immorality sins against his own body. Or do you not know that your body is the temple of the Holy Spirit who is in you, whom you have from God, and you are not your own? For you were bought at a price; therefore glorify God in your body and in your spirit, which are God's. (1 Cor. 6:18-20)

Kids today, even Christian kids, are confused by the conflicting messages they hear. Recently, *Time* magazine ran a cover story on "Kids, Sex and Values." The subtitle read: "Just do it. Just say 'No.' Just wear a condom." What is a teenager supposed to think? They hear one thing at home, another at church, another at school, and another through music and the media.

A one-hour special on MTV exemplified the ambiguities. Teenagers who were interviewed indicated that free choice was the determining factor. If somebody wants to have sex, that's cool. If somebody wants to be a virgin, that's cool too. That perspective sounds attractive, but it leads to emotional and hormone-based decisions. Young people need clear understanding of consequences of their behavior, both positive and negative, and they need good role models to follow.

Although physical drives, emotional needs, and peer pressures lure young people to experiment with their sexuality, kids seldom even consider the consequences beyond a passing thought. Pregnancy, disease, guilt, and a ruined reputation are problems for the other guy or gal. But kids can learn to make good choices. In the past couple of years, the Southern Baptists have joined with many other churches, denominations, and organizations to produce positive peer pressure and help young people make healthy decisions about their sexuality. This program, called *True Love Waits*, is a powerful influence in the lives of tens of thousands of young people.

Many young people desperately want guidance from their parents, extended family members, youth ministers . . . *anybody*! In his book *Right from Wrong* Josh McDowell reveals that 57 percent of evangelical church youth cannot affirm that an objective standard for right and wrong even exists. The air around them is filled with sexual messages. Parents need to take the initiative and help their kids distinguish the difference between right and wrong by talking to their teenagers about issues like: loving people instead of using them for personal pleasure, the physical and medical consequences of sexual promiscuity, the devastation of unwanted pregnancy, how promiscuity erodes self-confidence because people feel like sexual objects, how easy it is to develop a bad reputation and how difficult it is to change it, the law of diminishing returns, and how sexual immorality displeases God. These conversations should not be one-sided demands, however. Also, be sure to talk about how your teenager can obtain God's love, strength, and wisdom to handle the temptations. Teenage sexuality is a powerful force. Acknowledge the pressures and complexities. Listen to your teenager's concerns and questions without reacting. And pray for wisdom for both of you.

Dear Rodney,
My parents are both Christians and are both upstanding people in the community. Sometimes I feel that my parents get so caught up in their busy everyday schedules that they forget about their commitments as Christians and as parents/advisors. My mother and I are very close to one another but sometimes we get into an argument about her favoritism for my sister, who is seven years younger than me. I try to understand that my sister needs attention from my mom just like I do. The thing I need most from my mom is that she let me know that I can come to her anytime because there have been times which I need her judgement, but she wasn't there. As a result of that I have lost my virginity. I am not saying that it is her fault that I did what I did, but what I am saying is that if maybe I had had

someone to talk to I wouldn't have made the biggest mistake of my life.

What I need from my father is affection and love because I go looking for both of these things from boyfriends. I know it is not right to look for such deep emotional things in dates but I am a sensitive person who needs to at least be told once a day that I am loved. When I am not told that I am loved daily I get so depressed I think I will die. But despite these failures to communicate my feeling to my parents, I turned to God this week. I am also going to pray everyday that God will save my Christian spouse for me to marry someday.

Renee

Most parents have great difficulty talking to their teenagers about sexuality. I urge you: Don't cop out! If this topic is uncomfortable for you, ask your teenager to read this chapter and then talk about it. You can begin with less threatening questions such as, "Do the classes in your school teach the same things as this chapter?" or "How many of your friends know the things discussed in this chapter?" It is also appropriate to say, "You know, neither of us feel comfortable talking about sexuality, but I love you very much, and I want you to experience the very best God has to offer. I know the temptations are tremendous. And I'm sure some of your friends are experimenting, but I want to ask you to think about the facts in this chapter. They are hard, cold facts about the dangers of getting too involved. And these facts don't tell the half of it. They don't tell of the heartaches people experience and the deep regrets they carry when they lose their virginity, get pregnant, are used by others for sexual pleasures, or get terrible diseases. I'd like for you to talk to someone if you struggle with this area. I'd be glad for you to talk to me, but at least talk to someone—our youth pastor, your school counselor, your coach, or your aunt or uncle. Thanks for listening to me. I'd like to talk about this from time to time, not because I don't trust you, but because it is so important."

(Note: If you ask your teenager to read this chapter, you may want to cut this sample conversation out or she'll get wise to you!)

Reflection/Discussion Questions

1. What are negative influences on your teenager's perspective of sexuality?
2. What are positive influences?
3. In your opinion, what constitutes normal, healthy sexuality for a teenager (your teenager)? (Consider: clothes, makeup, conversation, behavior, friends, music, etc.)
4. If you could be sure he or she would listen, what would you like to say to your teenager about:
   - peer pressure
   - lack of information
   - media pressure
   - alcohol and drugs
   - early dating
   - the law of diminishing returns
5. How and when can you begin a conversation about sexuality with your teenager? (Look at the last paragraphs for suggestions.)

CHAPTER 8

. . . How My Friends Make Me Feel

Manic-depressive. That's how some parents describe their teenagers. These kids are sky high one minute and in the dumps the next. What's the story? Usually, this kind of mood swing occurs in relation to the acceptance or rejection by their friends. The powerful forces of self-doubt keep teens off balance, susceptible to the whims of the omnipotent peer group. Adolescents believe: "Whatever they say is *truth*. Whatever they want is *best*. Whatever they believe about me is *who I am*."

Teenagers are very easily controlled by their peer group because they are so eager to please them. They become virtual puppets, dancing to the pulled strings of acceptance and rejection. Sometimes the pull on the strings is obvious: "I love you" or "I hate you." But usually, the messages are more subtle and are interpreted by the peer group's own culture and language. For instance, one group of junior high school girls tell each other, "I hate you," but in their circle it means, "You're really cool." (No wonder parents have problems communicating with them!) And whether the messages are subtle or overt, clear or disguised, they are powerfully manipulative.

In these turbulent teen years, relationships change because individuals experiment with new behaviors and others react to them. Some choose to try alcohol or drugs; some experiment with sex or a different crowd. All of these changes force decisions for friends: to accept the new behavior or not accept it; to ignore it or to confront it. This letter is typical of many.

Dear Rodney,
My buddy had been my best friend for five or six years. Lately our friendship has really broken up because he started hanging out with some guys and drinking. My girlfriend has been getting jealous about lots of things, little things. And my friends are jealous of me and my girlfriend. We been together for about a year.
I feel real bad about my best buddy and me. I told him one time, "Hey, you don't need to be doing this stuff. I might even tell your dad. You might be mad at me for a while, but you'll probably thank me in the long run." But with him being my best friend, he got in a lot of trouble for his drinking. Now we aren't best friends any more. We broke up about two or three weeks ago. Last time he went out he got stoned. He's lying to his parents, saying he's going one place then going another.
I told him I was worried about him, but he didn't listen. He said he was mad at me because I wasn't drinking with him. I figured that if he's drinking and I'm around, then they're going to think I'm drinking too. He knows its wrong, but he doesn't care. At least that's what he says.
I wish we could be friends again.

Hector

People will do anything to get away from their problems. Rock idol Kurt Cobain, of the group Nirvana, sang of his bitter heartache in songs like *I Hate Myself and Want to Die*. He openly talked of his emptiness and his desire to commit suicide to end his pain. A *USA Today* cover story about Cobain's death commented: "An uneasy spokesman for disaffected youth, Cobain led a musical revolution with raw, punk-propelled grunge rock and an angst-filled voice that howled with the pain and rage of alienation. He captured the mainstream by not catering to it. But fame, wealth and even love could not heal the wounds of his shattered childhood in the logging town of Aberdeen, Washington, where he was passed around to relatives after his parents divorced when he was eight."[1] The tragedy of Kurt Cobain is not only this one man's pain and escape; the real tragedy is that many thousands of others so easily identified with his hurt and rage.

I'll never forget *People* magazine's cover story about Drew Barrymore. The title of the article read simply, "Little Girl Lost." The subtitle on the cover stated: "Drew Barrymore, the star of the movie *ET* at 7, started drinking at 9, smoking pot at 10, using cocaine at 12—now a teenager and in therapy." Barrymore's story was sensationalized because she is a star, but her problems are much like those of any other young person. When the interviewer asked her what she wanted most in life, she responded, "I just want to be accepted."

Young people are willing to do whatever it takes, and to risk whatever they have, to be accepted by their friends. When they can't seem to earn this acceptance, or if they fear losing this acceptance they've worked so hard to get, they become afraid. They feel alone, and they want to escape.

A few months ago, I spoke to a high school assembly in Alabama. After I finished, a lovely young lady waited to talk to me. She wore long sleeves even though the weather was very warm that day. She looked down at the floor as she began.

"Rodney, I feel so alone. You're probably wondering why I'm wearing this blouse. It's because I'm trying to hide the scars on my wrists. Just six months ago, I tried to kill myself."

"Why did you try to kill yourself?" I asked her.

She looked up at me and said slowly, "I just couldn't take it anymore. I tried so hard to fit in, but when I moved here, I just couldn't get into any of the groups of kids." She looked down again. "Now I fit in with the losers."

The control game is not just a one-way street. Your teenager will learn (and learn very quickly) to use these manipulative devices on others. Boys learn to act tough. Girls learn to act cool. Perhaps you've already noticed that your child has a new repertoire of expressions, gestures, and lingo designed to win approval, deflect rejection, and punish offenders.

Christian parents have to discern how much of their child's

peer focus is a normal part of the developmental process, and how much of it is destructive. If parents react too strictly, they may drive their child away. If they don't see manipulation, they won't have meaningful conversations about it with their child and the child may drift unnecessarily. Recognize that the peer group's approval is very important, but try to maintain good communication. Ask questions. Don't preach. Give suggestions sparingly.

The peer group focus is an intermediate step in the transition from looking to parents for answers to becoming self-reliant. As teenagers mature, they learn to make their own decisions about behaviors, people, and beliefs. Expect to see a gradual shift in later adolescence. If you expect it too soon, you will be disappointed, and you may put unrealistic expectations and pressures on your child.

Teenagers are sometimes vicious and cruel to one another. Your teenager will feel deeply hurt at times by those he now values most. When this happens, avoid the urge to be Mr. or Mrs. Fix-it. Teenagers don't want a lecture on the fickleness of friendship. They don't want you to call somebody and chew them out. They just want to know that you are there for them and that you care. That's all. That's enough.

One young lady wrote me about how her parents offered support and comfort when her friends hurt her.

Dear Rodney,
Some of my friends treat me like dirt, and it just makes me want to scream and cry my eyes out. Some of my friends talk about me behind my back. They tell me my hair looks bad when I think it looks good. They mock me. When ever I have some candy or some kind of food and I share it, they tell me the next minute "Oh wow, you hair looks good today!" but I know they don't mean it. It just hurts.
Sometimes I just go to my room and cry my eyes out about what they said about me that day. I hold it in all day when they keep on saying stuff about me like "Gosh, your hair is nappy. Run a brush through it," when I have just brushed my hair.
My parents on the other hand tell me everything that I am wearing that day looks pretty or nice. When my friends at school

say "You're a nerd." or "Why are your wearing that? It makes you look like a nerd." I try to hold it in all day. It really hurts, when they say something about me and I like that something about me. It makes me feel I'm getting smaller and smaller every time they say something about me.

My parents ask me every day "How was you day, dear?" I feel like telling them what really happened, but instead I just say "It was ok. It was really good."

Charlotte

Teenagers' cruel taunts inflict terrible pain. And sometimes, the teenager feels deep pangs of guilt. In a recent incident, a group of girls made fun of a loner who finally could not stand the pain and tried to commit suicide by running out into a busy street. One of the girls who taunted wrote me:

Dear Rodney,

We were making fun of her, my friends and I. We were saying it out of fun. Piggy, Ugly, and Dum were the only words we said to her, for she wasn't one of us. We didn't know the hurt she felt, we didn't know she wanted to kill herself. The boys in the parking lot were waiting for their rides. She was waiting also. One boy threw a rock at her, then another, then another, then they all joined in. Running, dashing, screaming was all she could do.

Then all of a sudden she ran into the street. She screamed. When the others realized what happened, they ran inside the building screaming, "She's been hit! She's been hit!" Chaos and confusion was all I remember then. I remember that she was in a coma and that she would never be normal again. She'll never have a chance to be a part of our group, and she'll never even have a chance to try. She'll never have a chance to be in any group.

I feel that I was a part of making it happen. I will always live with the feeling that I had a part in making her lose a chance to live a normal life.

Gwen

Teenagers' friendships will be the source of great pleasure

during these turbulent times, and they will be the cause of tremendous heartache. Sometimes this can occur in a single day, or even a single hour. Be aware of the volatility of these relationships and the tensions they create. Don't take any peer relationship for granted. It may change in a few minutes!

If you are concerned about the effect your child's friends are having on her, I suggest you:

- Talk to your pastor or youth pastor to gain perspective and advice.
- Talk to the school counselor to get his or her perspective of your child's peer relationships. You may find that the situation is better or worse than you thought.
- Talk to your teenager about the importance of choosing good friends. Be careful to explain that you respect her and you want her to make her own decisions. Express your concern without going into elaborate detail and without expressing much emotion. If you try to control her, you will probably push her more toward her undesirable peers.
- Find a good Christian summer camp for your child. In this environment, he will probably be surrounded by young men and women who are following Christ and having fun too! God uses these camps in tremendous ways to shape lives and give perspective to relationships back home.
- Ask a close relative to be a special friend to your child. An aunt or uncle may be able to communicate more deeply and honestly than a parent at this point because the relationship is less threatening. Advice, then, is more readily received.

Parents hope and pray for good friends for their children. These friends can have a powerfully positive impact on our teenagers, lead them to Christ, nourish them in their faith, and strengthen them in difficult times. All parents of teenagers would be happy to read letters like this one.

Dear Rodney,
My parents don't understand why I'm always at church. My friends makes me feel accepted. They build my self-esteem. They

help me feel wanted and I hope that I make them feel the same way. They are people I can trust and I can tell them my secrets. They are with me through the ups and downs of my life. They give me moral support. I can ask stupid questions, and they don't make fun of me. I do their hair and mess it up and we all laugh. We talk to each other and pray with each other.

Pat

Reflection/Discussion Questions

1. Who are your teenager's best friends? Describe the families of each of these friends.
2. What influences do these friends have on your teenager? How do you know?
3. Which of these resources can help your teenager develop positive, wholesome friendships? Explain how the ones you choose can help your teenager.
   - pastor or youth pastor
   - school counselor
   - encouragement to spend time with certain people
   - summer camp
   - asking a relative to spend time with him or her
4. What kinds of communication will be counterproductive and drive your teenager away from you and the kind of friends you value?

CHAPTER 9

. . . What I Like about Mom and Dad

Dear Rodney,

My parents are wonderful! They provide my brother, sister, and me with everything we could want or need. Of course, we have our moments with each other. There are many days that we lock horns over the littlest things. Sometimes I get so angry and hurt, I feel that they will stop loving me for good. This feeling doesn't last long, and when we "make up," we embrace in tears and tell each other how much the other means.

My parents don't have to embrace me to show their love for me. I have found that the best ways they show their love for me are by "the little things" they do. I always feel special when my father comes home from work tired and hungry but still helps me polish my guitar. Sometimes he'll save an article from a magazine that he knows I'd enjoy reading. The older I get, the more I cherish these small favors over the large gifts we get at Christmas.

Unfortunately, I often overlook these little things. I sometimes forget to thank my parents even though I am appreciative of them. I don't mean to hurt them or appear ungrateful because I am very grateful. But I never realized how much they sacrifice for me until long after it has happened.

Someday I will have children of my own. I hope I will be as good a parent to my children as my parents have been to me. I also hope I will remember to do "the little things."
Amy

Yes, it's true. If they think hard enough, most teenagers can think of things they like about their parents. They probably won't tell them, but they do. It isn't cool for most adolescents to be appreciative because that wouldn't reflect their growing independence. It is much more acceptable to the peer group to grouse and complain about the stupid rules their parents give to them. But deep inside, they genuinely appreciate the love and commitment of their parents.

Parents who are starved for any positive reinforcement from their teenagers need to learn to look for signs. The kids have their own language and signals. We are oblivious to most of them, but we need to learn to see the ones that are directed toward us. For instance, making eye contact and asking for advice communicates, "You are a safe person for me. I'm not supposed to like you, but I do."

Some adolescents break the stereotypical mold and communicate often and well with their parents. This occurs for one of two reasons: They may feel safe and secure and can grow gracefully toward independence. Or they may feel insecure and use their verbal skills to win their parents' favor. One behavior results from stability and strength, the other from fear.

Many people observe that teenagers learn to appreciate their parents again as they enter their twenties. By this time, they have learned many hard lessons, and as one young man said, "My parents aren't as dumb as I thought they were!" Hopefully, it won't take many years for your teenagers to communicate their appreciation for you. But in the meantime, you may need to learn to read their signals so you can understand their messages. Even then, you probably won't get all you want or deserve.

A family doesn't have to be perfect for teenagers to appreciate their parents. If kids feel they have their parents' ear, they feel connected and respected. In fact, going through hard times together by communicating clearly and often will strengthen the family bonds. This teenager's family went through tremendous stress, but she and her parents communicated and grew together.

Dear Rodney,

Even though I am only fifteen, family is very important to me. I guess my parents know I love them, but I don't think they realize just how much. A lot of things have happened between us, but through it all I have always loved them. I learned a long time ago that I will always love them.

My mom decided a couple of months ago, that she wanted to divorce my dad. So me and her talked and she said that she would try and stay and work it out. And so far things have been going great. I really admire my parents. My mother is a wonderful lady who is just like me. She got married when she was seventeen and never got the opportunity to go to college. I think when she was about thirty-four she decided to go back to school and further her education. Well, it's been five years since she started back; and since she was working a full time job it took her longer than she had first anticipated. This fall she will get her associate degree in criminal justice, then she plans to attend college in a program where she can obtain her bachelor's degree in two years.

I think the two best things about my mother are her determination and her strength. My mom isn't only my mother, she is my friend too. My father is a wonderful man. My father is a man who lives his dreams. He was in the Navy and went to a community college, but he still got an excellent education. My dad worked at a cabinet shop for eight years and hated every minute of it, but he only did it to support our family. I really admire my father for that. This man would go to Hell and back if it meant his wife and children were going to be happy. And last year my dad quit his horrible job to go into business for himself. Things might not be going to well right now, but God is working. I guess I get my passion for loving them from them. Because they loved me first. That's exactly why I love God. I am just so thankful that He gave me such wonderful parents. And for that I will always love Him.

Teri

Most teenagers notice most of what you do for them. (Yes, they really do!) It's just not cool to mention it. Remember, their job is to learn to be independent and to be wary of any and all authority, so they may not want to say anything embarrassing like, "Thanks!" But the old saying is true: When they get into their twenties, they'll become people again!

Still, some adolescents actually verbalize their appreciation for their parents.

Rodney,
I love my Mom and Dad so much because they have sacrificed so much for me. My Dad has worked extra jobs to help my Mom pay for Christian schooling for me because they care about me getting a good education. I could never say enough to say thanks to them. I remember the times when I was little and I had done something wrong and how my parents would punish me. They would say, "Now do you know why we are doing this?" and I would answer "Because you love me." I could see in their eyes how it would hurt them to have to punish me. But I always knew they loved me. I also remember when I was little how they made sure I was in Sunday School and at church activities. My Mom taught the lesson and I listened. Because of my parents I am a Christian now and have sold out to Jesus.
I think my parents are the best in the entire world and I would never want anyone else. So for my Mom and Dad, I love them, and I would never trade them for anything.
                                                                    Marty

Your children really appreciate it when you show them they are special. Little things mean a lot. They may not say anything, but they feel loved and affirmed when you care enough to spend time with them. This young woman wants to express her appreciation for her father even though she finds it difficult to put into words.

Dear Rodney,
Sometimes I find it very hard to express my feelings toward my Mom and Dad. I find it harder to talk to my Dad. I love my parents very much, but sometimes I don't tell them that I love them all the time, or I don't take the time to sit and talk with my Dad and to tell him the things that I like about him. I find it hard to

tell him that I look up to him very much, and I admire him so much for what he does and that he stands up for what he believes in. My Dad is a pastor and he puts up with a whole lot. Sometimes I just want to get up and yell at those people that just sit and criticize everything he does.

As I get older I think it gets harder, because when I was little, I used to be a "Daddy's girl." My Dad and I are very much alike, so sometimes we don't get along all the time. But I am trying harder to talk to him more and to tell him I love him, but sometimes its hard because I'm not a very affectionate person. We go out on a "date" every Thursday morning before he takes me to school so sometimes we get to talk for a while.

Bonnie

Teenagers are vitally interested in spiritual things. Millions of them search for God and become believers each year, and the most positive influence on many of them is their parents.

Dear Rodney,

I want my parents to know how thankful I am for them. They showed me the right direction for my life. As I look around and see the bitterness, the hurt, and the pain other teens face from their abusive parents, I realize how much the Lord has blessed me.

I just don't understand why I've been given so much from my family. I know I don't deserve my godly parents, but I'm extremely grateful that He chose them for me.

It's hard for me to comprehend myself without my parents and what I'd be like. When I feel like the whole world is against me, my parents are there to comfort me and show me their love. At school each day, I feel like I live in a battlefield. Sometimes I feel like giving up, but my parents keep me going.

When I get up every day and go to the kitchen for breakfast, I see my Mom in the living room praying. Her prayers have helped me and encouraged me through a lot of tough times.

I just can't express in words how special my mom and dad are to me. Even if it sometimes seems like I don't love them, I do love them and appreciate all they've done for me.

Shannon

Dear Rodney,
Throughout life everyone is faced with the problem of growing up.
My parents are two people who have meant more to me than
anyone else during the journey through my teenage years. I can
look at the past, the present, and the future and know that because of them I am loved.
Both of my parents grew up in Christian homes. The godly foundation their parents helped build served as a stepping stone toward being the parents they are for me. Both my mother and my
father could look at their parents as examples. My mom saw the
qualities in her parents that she wanted to develop, and she
worked hard to be all that God meant for her to be. My dad
looked to his parents too. Together, my parents observed my
grandparents. They saw the characteristics and actions that
they liked, and they learned from the errors of my grandparents.
My parents were wise to make the past both an example and a
tool to learn from.
As I grew up and faced different challenges in my life, I noticed
that my parents are always willing to listen and give advice. They
support me a lot. My friends are always welcome, and I'm proud
to have them come to my house.
My parents never hide their love for each other. I don't think their
honeymoon has ended after twenty-one years! They both love Jesus too. Their love for God has made me want to follow Him too.
I'm excited about the future. I'm looking to my parents as examples for me to follow. I hope my children see me the same way I
see them. I know my parents will always be praying for me. I can
count on them to love and support me no matter what.

                                                          Lane

Teenagers realize that many of their friends and classmates live
in broken homes or homes which are full of tension and resentment. Stability may be an abstract concept, but many adolescents
greatly appreciate the security and stability their parents provide.

Dear Rodney,
I love my parents so much. They have been married for twenty-
two years. My mom was seventeen years old and my dad was

twenty-one years old when they got married. They have been together this long and survived. That is another thing I like about
them: They try really hard to make their marriage work. And
they work to support our family. My dad owns his own business.
No one works for him, but sometimes my sister and I help out.
I love my parents so much!

Rachel

Some teenagers even understand and appreciate the rules their
parents have for them! They seem to instinctively know that
these guidelines protect them from harm.

Dear Mom and Dad,
I don't often admit how much you mean to me, Mom and Dad. I
love the way you listen to me, even when you know I'm wrong. Letting me express myself often helps me see more clearly where I'm
wrong. Sometimes it seems I'm arguing just for the sake of arguing, but I'm not. I want to see where my limits are, I want to know
if you love me enough to say "NO."
Sometimes I'll beg you to let me do something I know is wrong, I
just want you to tell me I can't do it. Mom, as much as I gripe
and complain about curfews and rules, I really appreciate them.
You love me enough to set boundaries and limits so I don't get
hurt. I know I yell "You don't understand!" but you know what? I
don't understand either, so you're in good company.
I love the way you encourage me without pushing, and ask without nagging (most of the time). I wish I could tell you I love you,
and then prove it with my actions.
I love you, Mom and Dad.

Casey

Dear Rodney,
My parents are very dear Christian parents. So many times I
look back and see how much they love me. Sure, there are times
when they discipline me and I don't understand. Even when I was
little I had questions like "why did I get a spanking?" "Why can't I
have that?" And then I got a little older and I asked, "Why can't I
date until I'm sixteen? Why can't I go out with them? Why can't I

*go to his house even though his parents aren't there? You trust
me, don't you?"*

*Now I know the answers to those questions. My parents are
gradually helping me grow to one day be a godly Christian lady.
Yes, they trust me — that is hardly an issue. They know what's
best for me. I couldn't have everything I wanted when I was little
because then I would have to have the even bigger, more harmful
things when I was older. They spanked me because they loved me
and wanted me to know they cared. I couldn't date because that
just took that much more pressure off me when I was older. I
couldn't go out with "them" because they weren't healthy influences on my life. I may not have liked our rules then, but now I'm
glad I had them. It has made all the difference in my life and now
my parents and I are friends as well as family.*

I am grateful to God for my mother and dad!

Andrea

Your teenager may or may not be as expressive as those who
write these letters. If not, consider being the example of appreciation. Look for things in your teenager to appreciate, then
mention these traits. It is best if you can point out character
qualities such as honesty, integrity, helpfulness, loyalty, friendli-
ness, gentleness, cheerfulness, and bravery. You can appreciate
athletic and academic performance, but it is even more important
to value character qualities.

Don't make too big a deal of it, and for Pete's sake, don't say it
in front of their friends (unless you get permission first)! Play it
cool and straight, and your teenager will be encouraged by your
genuine affirmation. Sooner or later, she may even thank you for
something.

This young teenager wrote a poem to express her appreciation
for her parents.

Legacy

*My parents are the basis of my life.
Although at times I may not show it,
I love them dearly.*

Without them, I wouldn't be here.
They laugh with me through the good times.
Like at New Years, when all our family and friends get together.
They see me through the bad times.
Like when my grandma died.
Their love is endless,
And so is mine.
I'm glad my parents are who they are.
I love them to this day.
Sometimes, I may not be the best daughter,
But we love each other anyway!

Molly

Reflection/Discussion Questions

1. How did you feel as you read this chapter? Explain.
2. What are some things you liked about your parents when you were a teenager?
3. What are some ways you can begin the cycle of appreciation in your family?
4. What are five specific things you can do to demonstrate your love and attention to your teenager?

CHAPTER 10

. . . What I Can't Stand about Them

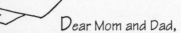

Dear Mom and Dad,

I'm tired. I'm sick and tired of trying to impress you. I've made the grades, I've won the awards, I hung around the right people, I gone out with the boys you've wanted me to, I've been as straight as I can, and I've made you proud of me. But I'm tired of you always changing my mind for me. Well now I think I'm old enough to make my own decisions. I'm really sorry that I don't measure up to your expectation.

Your daughter

OK, this is what you expected (and feared), isn't it? They can't stand the way you scowl at them when they won't tell you the whole story of why they were late getting home. They can't stand your nagging and your criticisms. They can't stand the fact that you want more than they want to give. Or they can't stand the fact that your spouse is too preoccupied with work to demonstrate interest and love.

Adolescents desperately need stability and security at home. They see their friends' families fall apart and hear the horror stories of divorce or drug abuse or physical abuse. And they are afraid it will happen to them . . . if it hasn't already. Turmoil in their bodies and minds, pressures at school, and stories from their friends leave them vulnerable and needy. And vulnerable people are often very angry people.

As I have traveled across the country, I have heard thousands of young people tell me about their anger. Here are some of the reasons for their rage.

Critical Parents

Teenagers attempt a lot of new things. They live by trial and error. Some parents, however, can't cope with the "error" part of that equation, and they constantly point out every transgression of their lofty expectations. Sadly, this nagging becomes a habit for many, and soon, the only way these parents know how to relate to their teenagers is to criticize.

Psychologists tell us that people need to hear at least ten positive comments for each corrective one. In many families, this ratio is reversed. And in some, the teenagers haven't heard a word of affirmation in years.

Out of Control Parents

Few things are more devastating to a child than parents out of control. One young man sadly told me, "All my dad does is yell at me and my sister. From the time he walks in the door, he comes unglued and yells at us. I know I mess up, but not *that* much!" The young man's expression changed to anger, "I hate him! I wish he would drop dead!"

Parents may be out of control in many ways. Some parents are so depressed they can't take care of their responsibilities, so the children have to become surrogate parents. Some parents are violent—hitting, throwing things, and cursing. Even if a child isn't the victim, she lives in fear that she will be the next time. She is a passive victim of that parent's violence.

I heard from one teen who felt this way.

Dear Rodney,
I hate my step-dad when he says "I'm not her dad." He doesn't

even want to be associated with me. And I hate him when he shows favoritism toward my brother. Sometimes he gives me a chore my mother already gave my brother,

I wish my mother knew how much I hate it when she gets two inches in my face and screams at me. I also hate when she calls me five different times the minute I go up and down those stairs. And the most thing I hate is when they promise me something and then they don't follow through.

I can't wait to be gone from here.

Emily

Some parents are addicted to a substance or a behavior. Their primary need is satisfying their craving. The children become secondary, and they know it. The addiction, however, is only the tip of the iceberg. Underneath are wrenching emotional forces which destroy lives. One young man wrote me:

Rodney,

My father is a real bad alcoholic. When I was a kid, he beat me all the time. Me, my brothers and sisters. Now we live with my grandmother. He got a divorce from my real Mom. And now I don't even know where she is or what her name is. My mom kept saying it's OK, it'll get better, but it just kept getting worse. Many times, if I'd had a gun, I would have just taken my life right there. I just couldn't go on. I still wake up at night thinking about it—flashbacks, bad dreams.

A lot of the time I feel like it's my fault—that I did something I shouldn't of. I never see my Mom, and I only see my Dad every now and then. He still drinks. I won't go around him. When he comes to visit us, I go somewhere else because I know if I try to talk to him, it won't do any good.

Maybe it is my fault. Maybe if I had been a better son they would have been nicer to me. Sometimes I think that I might do something like that to my children (If I ever have any), and I hate it. I hope I don't treat my son the way my Dad has treated me.

Marvin

Some parents are so busy fixing other people's problems, they don't even notice the needs in their own children's lives. Some are church workers who get strokes for being teachers, deacons, or youth volunteers, but neglect their own families.

Dear Rodney,
My parents would be more understanding if they had a clue of how I feel about them. Our family really isn't a family. We all go our separate ways. We don't even eat dinner together. I hate staying at home because when I do I always get fussed at about how we don't do anything together.

Now, my parents are Christian people. My dad use to work with the youth. My mom and dad both love Jesus Christ. They have raised my two brothers and I to believe in Christ and to always do what we think Jesus would like. We use to go to church every time the doors open. But since my oldest brother got married and the other one went off to college we haven't been a family.

Now that both of my brothers are back home to live, they are always to busy for me or to stay home. Me and my youngest brother are closer. We talk, cut up, and go out together. There are four years difference in us. But my oldest brother and I don't talk. He is eight years older. I always try to get him to do something with me, but he is always too busy.

I love my family with all my heart. When I try to have a family night something always goes wrong. Every time it never fails one of my brothers have something else to do. So I always end up watching a movie.

My dad and I can go out and have the best time. Just the two of us.

My parents don't ever go out together. Very much. That's sad. My dad invites my mom to do things but she always has better things to do like sit down, watch TV, and smoke—which irritates the stew out of me!

I just wish that one day I will be able to sit down with them and talk like a real family does.

Raymond

Strict Parents

Some parents who feel out of control try to impose rigid rules and high expectations on their children. Subconsciously, they may be trying to compensate for their own needs. Or perhaps they simply can't stand one more area of life that causes them problems, so they put the clamps on the kids to be sure they don't mess up.

Some strict parents give rules and mete out judgment for transgressions from a distance. Others hover over their kids and smother them with controlling attention, telling them everything to say, think, do, and be. A common complaint from teenagers is, "My parents treat me like a kid!" Clearly, they resent it! They are becoming adults and want (demand) to be treated like adults.

Dear Rodney,
I can't stand alot of things about my parents. Like how they still treat me like I'm about the same age as my little ten yr. old brother. How they hardly let me do anything. Also how my dad is such a jerk to my mother and me. He treats us like crap while he does just about everything for my brother. He's always coaching him in every sport. How he sits on his butt and talks on the phone all day, and then complains about how we have no money. Then I can't stand how my parents are always around. And most of the teachers know who they are. I mean it was ok when I was younger, but not now. They're always around, and I can't stand it anymore. They want to know why I stay in my room all the time or out with my friends and never home. I just wish they'd leave me alone unless I want to be around them.

                                          Lewis

Dear Rodney,
Sometimes I can't stand my parents. They treat me like a little kid sometimes. If I ask them for something, they tell me that's what I get allowance for. On the allowance I get, I'll never to be able to buy anything. My parents are also overprotective. One thing I really can't stand is when my mother gives my stuffed animals to Goodwill. I collect stuffed animals. They make good

friends because they don't tell your secrets, they don't use you, and they don't care if you cry on them for two hours. But my mother gives them away!

My parents get mad at me too easily. That makes me mad. Well, these are just a few of the things that I can't stand about my parents. If I wrote everything, it would be a novel.

Frances

Dear Rodney,

If I told my parents why I can't stand them, they would probably be somewhat upset but I think they'd understand. I can't stand my parents because of many reasons. One of them is, I hate it when I say I did something wrong and their first reaction is either "You're grounded!" or "You bet you did something wrong!" Another thing is they never trust me. They always ask if I did something, such as a chore, and when I say "yes," they ask if I did it that day at that time. Why can't they just trust me? I wish they'd just treat me like a person instead of a thing.

Rob

Indifferent Parents

On the other extreme, some parents are so absorbed in their own problems, they don't give attention, love, and instruction to their kids. They may live in the same house, but the children are basically on their own, emotionally abandoned by one or both of the parents. Teenagers may say they want their parents to leave them alone, but they certainly don't want to be abandoned during this pivotal time in their lives. They want and need attention, affirmation, and guidance.

Young people often complain that their parents are inconsistent. They use the word *hypocrisy*—pretty strong language for pretty strong emotions. To these teenagers, parents who are inconsistent communicate parents who just don't care enough to be honest. These letters are representative.

Dear Rodney,

My father is very hypocritical, and is always in a bad mood. My father always embarrasses me and my friends, especially in front of girls. And he is very old fashioned. For example, he likes old cars and trucks and always says he was born a hundred years too late. He sometimes says he wishes he lived one thousand miles from nowhere all alone.

My mother is a very nice person but she is very protective of me. Sometimes she won't let me drive or other things.

But all in all both my parents try hard, love, and take care of me. My dad is always telling us how easy we have it "Nowadays." Because when he was young his family was poor, and he had to work on the family farm. Every time I am bothered by something he always has had it worse and thinks nothing of my problems, except that they are trivial little problems with almost no importance, but somehow and in someways I understand, because I know some of what he has to go through at work; and I would be ill too.

And he is always in a bad mood, and he always yells at me, especially when I drive. What he doesn't know is that his yelling just makes it worse.

My mother isn't that bad, but she won't let me go as much as my dad.

My father always makes fun of me because I can't do something he can. Actually it is more like a scolding, because he thinks I act helpless on purpose.

Donald

Dear Rodney,

My parents have had a bad influence on my attitude. They are separated from each other. My mother lives in Ft. Worth, my father in Tyler. But even distance cannot settle the hatred between them. They're both Christians but have no foundation for their beliefs. They tell me to love others, when they can't show Christian love between themselves. They tell me to watch my attitude when they're the ones that cannot control their anger with each other. If my parents wouldn't be so hypocritical, it'd make life a whole lot easier!

Pepper

Dear Rodney,
I watch my parents real closely. Everyday it seems my parents fall in their walk a little further each time, only to go rock bottom each week and then make a pilgrimage to church to clear things up with God to be able to foul things up again next week.
I just don't get it. WHY? Why can they do whatever they want and it be okay? "Because I'm the mommy!" Sorry excuse. Furthermore, why would anyone want to do that? It hurts, really hurts, to have your closest Christian influence telling you that its okay to live a life of sin because they're adults.
Did I miss something? Sometime after you've had a baby, does somebody walk up and say "Congratulations, now you can sin?!" No!! A thousand times no!
But day and night, week after week of stinking hypocrisy. I can only pray. I am not allowed to reprimand or scold or punish; because I'm not the mommy and I'm not the daddy.

Barbara

Divorce

A seventh-grade boy looked troubled. "Dad," he began slowly, "are you and Mom ever going to get a divorce?"

His father was surprised because he and his wife had a strong relationship. "No, son, we've made a commitment for life. Why do you ask?"

"Well, a lot of kids in my class have parents who are divorced, and I just wanted to know if you and Mom might get divorced too."

Even in strong homes, the fear of family break-up leaves many children insecure. It's no wonder. Half the marriages in the country break up. And this statistic doesn't communicate the amount of confusion and fear in the hearts of children from divorced families and nondivorced families alike. These children don't want to be cut off from vital relationships. They don't want to watch the hatred and game-playing which forces them to take sides. They don't want to be made to like people who have taken the place of their real mom or dad or siblings in blended families.

Multiple Households

Many kids feel the strain of being in one household one weekend and a different one the next. They need stability and continuity, but they live in constant change. They are forced to figure out and find their place in multiple-family systems, and the dynamics of each may be completely different.

Two-Career Families

The desire for more income and opportunities for women outside the home have led to rapid growth in the number of mothers in the work force. Sometimes this may be necessary, but it is often at the expense of the children who need the time and attention of at least one parent who isn't preoccupied and tired from work.

Embarrassment

When parents are out of control, the teenagers risk embarrassment. "My friends would laugh and tell me they saw my Dad drunk and asleep in his car on the side of the road again," one girl told me. "I just laughed with them, but I felt so ashamed!"

Teenagers also feel embarrassed when they have to tell their friends that they can't do something because their parents are too strict. "They treat me like a little child!" a seventeen-year-old young man said in disgust.

Another source of embarrassment is parents who don't know when to be invisible. Teenagers need to be independent, so parents need to realize what it does to a teen to be given instructions or correction in front of his peers. There is a time and place for everything. In the teenagers' peer-dominated world, parents must learn when to lay low and avoid embarrassment.

Favoritism

Adolescents have a very strong sense of justice, and they react in anger if they feel a sibling is given preferential treatment. Let's face it, a compliant seven-year-old is much easier to be around than a struggling, moody teenager. It is very easy to give more time, attention, and affirmation to the younger child (or any child who is compliant, no matter how old he or she may be). And in disputes between the two, we naturally take the side of the compliant child. This may be natural, but it is deadly to the adolescent's sense of justice and fairness. Favoritism produces deep animosity in the people involved.

Catatonic Families

Teenagers may not want parents hovering around them, but they don't want corpses either. Some parents are so tired from work that all they want to do at home is relax. Others are so depressed, they want to escape. These parents may become "lounge lizards," mindlessly watching television for hour after hour to escape possible conflict in family communication. Kids often act like they want to be as far away from their parents as possible, but they want their parents to be available and *alive* when they do want to communicate.

Parents—even the very best ones—can't produce an environment so perfect that the children will never be angry. That's not the goal at all. Sometimes problems are unavoidable. The goal is to produce an environment in which each family member can talk honestly and safely about hopes and fears, hurts and joys. We grow, not by avoiding all problems, but by facing them with honesty, courage, and the encouragement of those who love us.

If you want to know what frustrates your teenager and what makes him genuinely angry, you can ask him questions like, "What do you like about our family?" or "What do you not like very much?" and "If you were me, how would you act as a parent?" When your teenager answers, bite your tongue. Listen carefully, and say something like, "Thanks for telling me. I'll try to do what you've asked me to do. Pray for me. And remind me next time I mess up again." If you do that, your tongue may have a hole in it, but your floor will be dented by your fainting teenager!

Reflection/Discussion Questions

1. Did you feel anxious as you read this chapter? Why or why not?
2. When you were a teenager, what did your parents do that angered you, frustrated you, or embarrassed you? How did you respond?
3. Are you afraid your teenager could have written one of the letters in this chapter? Why or why not?
4. Which of these factors create problems in your relationship with your teenager:
   - parents who are constantly critical
   - parents who are out of control
   - parents who are too strict
   - parents who are indifferent
   - divorce
   - multiple households
   - two-career families
   - embarrassment
   - favoritism
   - catatonic families

CHAPTER 11

. . . What I Believe about God and the Church

Dear Rodney,

If my parents really knew how I felt about God and Christianity they would probably freak! I've been born in a Christian and godly home and taught about Jesus my whole life. My parents tell me I was saved when I was four years old, but I don't remember that at all. There's so much that I don't believe about God and Bible. So much that I think isn't fair and doesn't make since.

My family has been going through many troubles and heart-aches recently with my older brother Ben. For several years now he has put our family through alot. Ben is very smart and a good guy but has fallen in with the wrong crowd. He has been kicked out of two schools in the last year, run away from home many times and even lived in a delinquent home for a while. My brother lives back at home now but still doesn't get along with my parents. My brother's lifestyle is still very wild. Among other things he is a local drug dealer, though he claims he doesn't use them himself.

I say all that to say, the main cause of many of their problems was religion. My parents are way too religious and have way too many rules. They believe in God too much. I really can't see much of anything God has done for them. But still they keep their faith in Him and always pray. It's ridiculous!

I really wish I could talk to my parents about this—how I feel and all. They would be very, very surprised. To them, I'm a nice, Christian girl who is a pleaser and does everything right. I'm a straight-A student and go to church every Sunday. I really wish they knew how I felt. But I really would be afraid of what they'd do to me. Plus I love them so much I would never want them to go through the pain and hell my brother put them through. But I don't believe how they believe. I just can't accept how a loving God could put all the pain and hurt in life that He does. Especially for those, like my parents. That doesn't make a whole lot of sense to me!

I've never told this to anyone—how I really feel—it feels good to get it out! Thanks!

Julie

Christian parents are sometimes aghast when their kids suddenly blurt out, "I'm not sure I believe that God stuff anymore. It sounds like a fairy tale to me." Questioning authority in the spiritual arena is, like the questioning of all authority, a normal part of adolescence. Kids experiment with different beliefs just as they experiment with different friends, sports, hobbies, clothes, and behaviors.

Many Christian kids feel confused during this time. The "smart people" at school—the intellectuals—tell them the Bible isn't true and that evolution is a fact. And they look around and notice that some of the most outspoken Christian students are, well . . . nerds. The social hierarchy doesn't value nerds, so that produces yet another tension. Now that they are older, they don't go to Children's Church anymore. They have to go to the main service, and it's boring. And many of the cool kids don't go to church at all. With all of these factors, the teenager's experience is not so much a crisis of faith as it is a crisis of fitting into their peer group.

Some adolescents test themselves and their parents by suddenly adhering to new beliefs. Teenagers are usually very spiritual, but they are exposed to all kinds of weird and sensational beliefs in the lunchroom at school, on campouts, and on bus trips. Actually, the adolescent years are a time of constant transition, so if a teen pronounces faith in some strange doctrine or deity, you will be wise to ask questions and listen instead of angrily condemning the foolishness of this experimental faith. Tomorrow, your teen may return to "the God of his fathers" if he doesn't feel forced into believing a certain way.

The searching, probing, experimenting nature of adolescence leads many to a sincere faith in Christ. In fact, some studies indicate that as many as 80 percent of Christians came to Christ during their teenage years. That incredible statistic makes youth ministry one of the most (maybe the most) important ministries of the church.

During the adolescent years, people make some of the most important decisions of their lives. They decide who will be their *master*, what will be their *mission* in life, and possibly, who will be their *mate*. These are idealistic, enthusiastic years in which young people dream great dreams and set the course of their lives. The search may temporarily take them far afield, but many will find their way to a strong, deep faith in Christ.

The role of a significant adult is vitally important in their decision-making process. Often, teenagers don't want to hear from their parents, but they will readily hear even the exact same message from a teacher, youth pastor, aunt, or uncle. Many churches are pouring time, talent, gifted people, and other resources into their youth ministry because they recognize these young, wild, and crazy people are making monumental decisions which will affect themselves, their families, the church, and the community for many years to come. It is the best investment a church can make!

Some teenagers wrestle with purely theological problems, but many have already experienced deep emotional wounds. Their questions about life, purpose, and God come from hurt, anger, and confusion. This young person's view of God was distorted by her relationship with her parents.

Dear Rodney,
Well I come from a single parent family. And have two sisters that are merryed. And a ex-step sister that i love very much. I live with my mom, And i'm not home too much cause of my mother working, But if my Mom only knew how lonely, and sad, and mad i am at God sometime for letting me feel this away.

*I know he loves me. But i feel lonely because i think God has
taken many loved ones from my life. First there was my real
mom and Dad that i was adopted from. Then there my step Dad
that i called Daddy and love very much. Then my Mom and Daddy
got a divorce and i had to stop seeing my Dad for about two
and a half years. I was hurt so bad because i was Daddy's little
girl. But now i feel so distant from him when we do talk, even
though he's still a loving and kind man.*

*Then after they devorce, my mom and Buddy got merry, so i had
to start all over again with a new family. it was scarey. a different feeling. After nine year of merriage, they got devorice. I was
hurt, and it seem to be all my fault because Buddy said and did
things he should'nt of done.*

*My step sister was one of the hardest thing to let go of. So now
i'm fourteen and alone and confused and just wish my mom had
an answer for me. I just don't know why God would take my loved
ones from me and hurt me so much. And i know I'll have the
chance in heaven to ask him myself, and i know God loves me.*

Beth

Many of the kids who talk to me after I speak at their school,
church, or youth camp express heartfelt desires for their parents
to have a vital relationship with God. Their genuine concern for
their parents' spiritual lives is both heartwarming and sad. Their
love for their parents and their evangelistic zeal makes me believe
there is real hope for that generation, but the lack of parental,
spiritual role models is alarming. Three kids wrote me about their
desires for their parents to come to Christ and follow Him.

Dear Rodney,
*I'm the only one in my family that goes to church. I am fifteen
years old. I often wonder if my parents are Christians and have
asked them many times. They say they are, but their lives don't
reflect it. When you came to my church, Rodney, you had a time
for families to come to the front and pray together. I felt like I
was the only one left that didn't have a family to pray with.*
*I really wish my parents would get involved with the Church.
There are many times that I think that coming to church together would bring us closer, but church only comes between us.*

I have so many strong Christian friends at church that are fun to be around, but my family feels I spend more time at church than with them.

God and the Church are so important to me and I wish they were as important to my family.

Tim

Dear Rodney,

My whole religious background is odd I guess. My mom was the only one in her family that went to church, and she went to the Epispocal church. My dad, on the other hand, was raised in a Baptist church. I don't really know the whole story but apparently he didn't want to be Baptist. Anyway, when they got married (in the Episcopal church) I guess they didn't think about how they would raise their children. Religiously that is.

I went to church with my Mom and sister at St. Luke's Episcopal for eight years. My dad decided he wanted us to go to church as a family but he didn't want to be Episcopal . . . so we joined a Methodist church. I was young so I don't really know what happened. But we quit going.

I went to a baptist church with a friend which is where I am now. I'd always thought I was saved, but wasn't sure till a camp in eighth grade. I got baptised and have been going here ever since. I guess my point in this long drawn-out story is: I want to share with my parents my thoughts on God, church, and religion, but I'm not sure how to go about it. I want them to tell me what they believe. I want to tell them what I believe. I'd like to pray with my family too, but that's never been a part of our family life. If they knew the big impact it is to me . . . maybe they would.

Lori

Dear Rodney,

Too many times today, parents put the responsibility on children to be the spiritual leader at home, or force them to go to someone else to get answers for Biblical questions. I mean, just think how many children don't get a strong Godly influence at home. They have to rely on themselves to find a way to get to church or to find a person they can talk to. Today there are so *many single parents, it's astounding. I wish parents would be more interested in helping us learn about God.*

Beverly

Expect your teenager to have serious questions about life, faith, and God. In fact, maybe you should be concerned if he doesn't. It is the nature of young people to question, to probe, to wonder, and to experiment. When your kid says, "Dad, I'm not sure I believe in God anymore," don't explode with, "What? I can't believe you could say such a thing!" followed by a lecture on the authority of Scripture, the deity of Christ, and the validity of the Dead Sea scrolls.

A more appropriate response would be, "That's very interesting. You know, people have wrestled with this issue for thousands of years. Have you read some of the scholars' writings?" (He probably heard it from another kid at lunch, but give him the benefit of the doubt.) Instead of interrupting and condemning, enter into the pursuit of truth with your teenager. Become a partner. Read Josh McDowell's Evidence That Demands a Verdict, and ask your teenager to read excerpts too. Chances are, your son will forgot about his earthshaking statement a few minutes after making it. Maybe it was just a passing thought. Maybe it was an attempt to "get your goat." Or maybe it was a statement of sincere reflection and honest pursuit of truth. If you are willing to accept your teenager and his questions, you can have some marvelous conversations.

Reflection/Discussion Questions

1. Describe your spiritual experience when you were a teenager.
2. How would you respond to your teenager questioning God and the Bible?
3. What are some positive spiritual influences in your teenager's life?
4. What are some negative influences?
5. What are some casual ways you can talk to your teenager about faith and truth?

PART 3

Encouragement
for Parents

CHAPTER 12

Learn to Listen

Teenagers pour out their hearts to me. I guess they perceive I'm not going to condemn them for having problems, and I'm not going to give them quick, easy advice that doesn't work in the real world. And many of them would pour out their hearts to their parents, too, if they were assured their parents would listen. Here are some heartbreaking letters I've received.

Dear Rodney,
I go to bed at night and tears always start flowing. I feel that my relationship with my father is horrible. My father and I hardly ever agree. It seems that no matter how hard I try, everything is wrong in his eyes. I want to please him, but I can't.
My mother almost always takes my sister's side. It seems like I'm not loved. We never do anything together or talk to each other. Things are awful.
My sister and I are seven years apart. We have nothing in common. She is cute and adorable (of course, I'm not). The one thing we both have, though, is our stubborn attitude. We both go our own separate way and our way only.

I wish my parents and my sister knew how much I love them. I'll say right now that I love them with all my heart.

Sara

Dear Rodney,

I wish my Mom knew how angry I get at her! I don't understand why we fight so much. She never understands me and she doesn't open up to me. She makes me feel so sad. And all I ask from her is to love me. I try so hard to do things to please her. I have cried and cried so many times.

I pray to God to keep her safe and for me not to lose love for her. But it's so hard to love someone you hardly know. I mean I know her face, but not her heart, and that's where I want to be. I wish she knew how angry I am at her for taking my father away from me.

I care so much for them both, and I want them both in my life. I long to be a family again. Sometimes it's so hard not to think about taking my own life but I know deep in my heart I wouldn't be just hurting myself but my family.

I thank God for giving me the strength to help change my mother's heart and turn her eyes to Jesus. I get so angry when she talks about people she doesn't know. I don't understand her, but I know deep in my heart she may one day meet the Lord, but if she doesn't change I wouldn't want her to be with the Lord.

Philip

Dear Rodney,

My mom and my real dad had a divorce before my first birthday. My mom, following her divorce, got married to my Step Dad. This is the man I've known throughout my life as my real dad, seeing how contact with my real father has been scarce. Anyways, my mother has always been there for me, and I love her greatly. I have always lived with her until my fifth and sixth grade year. Then she moved to Ohio for certain reasons. I then lived with my father in Texas.

Eventually, I moved to Ohio to live with her and grew very close to my friends and her boyfriend's kids. When I say close, I mean I could open up to these people and felt a lot of love for each one of them. Well, I came back to Texas this summer and ended up staying because of family I sincerely missed, especially my cousin Shawn who I had grown up with all my life. I now want to move back, but I also want to stay for obvious reasons.

I am so confused about what to do. This makes me angry at my family because each one makes me feel guilty when I choose to live with the other. I just want them to know that I need their support and understanding in my decisions because it makes me feel guilty when they don't give it to me. It is hard enough with all the other pressures of life, such as making good grades, staying out of drugs and sex, etc. I just wish that somehow I could talk to them about this, without feeling like I'm in an awkward position.

Kay

Dear Rodney,

Whenever I have a problem, I feel like I have no one to talk to. I know I have God and that should be enough, but sometimes it's not. Everyone makes me feel like I always have to be happy. Since I am outgoing and cheerful, I always have to act like this or everyone acts differently around me. It's like I am all alone, and that I alone must solve my problems.

If my parents understood how I feel then maybe they could help me with my problems so that I don't have to hide my feelings.

Cheryl

Most parents make the mistake of telling first and listening second (if at all). Understanding and communication, however, are not attained by demands for compliance. Listening is an art form which any of us can acquire if we are willing to practice reflecting and clarifying what is said by others. Quite often with teens, the issue isn't the issue—that is, they don't really care what you think of the issue you are discussing with them. They only want to see if you will love them enough to listen to them and value their opinions. A teenager wrote me:

Dear Rodney,
I don't always go to my parents to talk about important issues in my life because most of the time I just want to get things "off my chest." But they always want to add something. It's like they can't stand for me to have any problem at all without them fixing it. But all I want is for them to listen! If I want their advice, I can ask for it. I'm not a ten-year-old anymore!
I wish they could just listen without having to have the last word.

Kevin

Reflecting is repeating to a person what he has just said to you in order to be sure you heard correctly. It doesn't imply any value judgment at all. You may say, "This is what I hear you saying," and repeat what you heard. This gives the person the opportunity to tell you, "Yes, that's what I said," or "No, you missed it. Let me try again."

Clarifying is asking follow-up questions to get a better understanding of the feeling or situation. You may ask questions like *who*, *what*, *when*, *where*, and *how*. Or you may use open-ended statements such as, "Tell me more about that." As you hear more, it often gives you (and the person who is talking) more insight into the situation. Recently, I talked with two eighth-grade girls about the problems both of them had with a mutual friend. I tried not to draw any conclusions as I asked them questions. For about thirty minutes, I asked and they talked, and by the end of the conversation, I had a very different impression of the situation than I did when we began. If I had given advice after the first five minutes, I would have been wrong, and the relationships may have been damaged.

As we reflect and clarify, we often come to a deeper understanding of the true nature of the problem, and we also gain our own realization of the solution. Self-discovery is actually better than being told the answers. It develops problem-solving skills and builds confidence.

Sometimes, people are so thrilled to have someone listening to them that they assume you agree with all they say because you aren't instantly condemning or correcting. A few months ago, I patiently listened to a young man blaming his problems on his dad. He talked for a while, and I asked him questions without giving advice. Then he looked intently at me, smiled, and said, "So you agree with me. That's great!"

"I didn't say I *agree* with you," I informed him. "Only that I *understand* you." But feeling understood opened the door for him to hear my analysis of his problem. I then asked him, "What would you advise someone in your situation to do?" The young man came up with ideas that were creative and astute. They were even better than the ones I had thought of.

In addition to reflecting and clarifying, you will need to use what I call *The Seven "BEs" to Good Listening*. They are:

1. Be Observant

Someone once told me: "Listen with your eyes as well as with your ears." Notice the facial expressions, posture, clothes, eye contact, and tone of voice. These may give a far better indication of the speaker's true condition than the words themselves.

2. Be Available

Sometimes teenagers come home late from a party and want to talk. If we mumble, "That's great. I'd love to hear about it in the morning," as we stumble off to bed, we may never hear what they wanted to tell us. Don't let the opportunity slip by. Talking to adolescents is much like fishing: It doesn't do much good to go when it is convenient. To catch fish, you have to go when the fish are biting!

3. Be Kind

Don't interrupt your teen's conversation to give advice, or worse, to condemn. Don't jump to conclusions out of fear of losing control. Ask questions and patiently listen.

Also, allow teenagers their own space for privacy. Their rooms need to be their domain. It needs to be cleaned every millennium or so, but when they close the door, no one should be allowed in without permission.

4. Be Demonstrative

Give hugs, kind words, and "I love yous" liberally to your teenagers, even if they seem like they don't want them. But be genuine, and don't use your affection to manipulate them into doing something for you. "Let love be without hypocrisy" (Rom. 12:9).

Spontaneous, unexpected gifts communicate love to people. These need not be expensive at all—even the smallest gift lets someone know that you were thinking of her.

5. Be Wise

Don't demand perfection. Parents can nitpick their kids to death. Look for many positives to address and only a few *major* negatives. It is counterproductive to nag about everything you see that could be improved. As the old saying goes, "We can't fight on every hill. We'd better choose our hill to die for!" There's another old saying: "Therefore be wise as serpents and harmless as doves" (Matt. 10:16). Both of these statement are worth remembering.

6. Be an Example

Thousands of teenagers attest to the devastating consequences of parents telling them, "Do as I say, not as I do." Whether it is drinking, drugs, illicit sex, lying, stealing, gossip, outbursts of anger, or any other bad behavior, children will follow our actions instead of our words. If our actions do not match our words, we lose credibility in their eyes, and we have done double damage.

Having children is a motivator toward getting us to examine our lives, repent, and follow righteousness. The responsibility of reproducing ourselves in the lives of our children is a heavy burden, but it can be one of the most fulfilling joys in life to see them follow Christ because they saw that example in us. In this case, *they* reap what *we* sow.

7. Be Courageous

Parenting adolescents is a tough job. It requires tenacity, tenderness, and courage. We need the strength to listen patiently, ask questions when we'd rather correct immediately, carefully explain our expectations, follow through with discipline, and affirm, encourage, and love these young people entrusted to us. Even when they may not appreciate it one bit!

The main reason people don't want to share with others is that they are afraid of the response. Good listening involves withholding judgments until the person feels heard and understood. Too often, we go ballistic. Listening is a skill. It can be learned and developed. It takes practice and coaching and trial and error, but all of us can learn to listen well.

Good listeners are respectful of others. Don't make fun of what another person says or condemn them for giving their opinion. Make eye contact and keep your body posture positive and open. Don't interrupt, either. Train yourself to say things like, "Tell me more," even when you disagree. You can say, "I don't agree with you, but we can disagree agreeably."

One of the hardest things to learn is awareness of your facial gestures and tone of voice. Gestures and voice tone can make or break a conversation. Think about somebody glaring at you saying, "Go ahead! Tell me more!" How would you interpret that request? I'd think they wanted more ammunition to blow my head off! But the same words can be spoken gently and with genuine concern. There's no question of which one I'd be more likely to respond to.

There may be any number of reasons why your teenager won't talk to you. She may be ashamed of something she's done and want to withdraw. He may be exhausted and unwilling to summon the energy to communicate. She may be angry with you and using silence to punish you. He may have picked up this behavior by watching his friends relate to their parents. She may be deeply depressed and uncommunicative. He may be deeply hurt by something you have said or done. She may be afraid you will take any shared information to someone who will hurt her. He may have gotten in a habit of not communicating with adults. She may, like all teenagers at times, simply need a little space and independence.

Sometimes we try to guess why our teenager isn't talking to us. And often our guess is wrong. These young people are going through tremendous changes. They need lots of love and affirmation, and they need some space too. When we guess at their needs instead of asking them, we can compound the problem—for them and us. You may need a checklist of options to consider before you jump to a conclusion. Often, parents believe (and fear) their children are thinking, feeling, and acting in exactly the same way they did when they were kids. This is called *projection*, and it is an unhealthy and unhelpful hindrance in communication.

Teenagers are difficult. They are selfish, moody, constantly changing, and full of inner turmoil. They play lots of relational games at school to get in with the right peer group. They learn to put others down. They learn the not-so-desirable skills of manipulating each other with anger, withdrawal, sarcasm, praise, and a full assortment of facial expressions. Then they try to use these at home. Don't be dragged into adolescent ways of communicating. Be direct, honest, and kind.

Most parents of teenagers complain about the lack of communication with their kids. Some have too much communication. Some parents, especially those who are deeply hurt by strained marriages or divorce, unconsciously try to have their own emotional needs met by their teenagers. Telling teenagers, especially younger teens, our deepest hurts and longings can distort the relationship. They feel like they have to be our peers. Or worse, the roles are reversed and the children become parents to us. Don't tell your teenager too much. Instead, find a close friend, pastor, counselor, or support group with whom to share yourself. And gain wisdom from these sources about how much is appropriate to tell your children. Certainly, they need to know some of how you think and feel—and they need to feel free to tell you about their needs—but telling them too much puts undue burden on them to comfort you and fix your problems. That isn't their role.

As I talk to teenagers all across the country, many of them tell me that they want to spend more time with their parents, especially their dads. They don't necessarily want to have the deepest talks in the world with them. They just want to feel close, connected, and a part of their parents' lives. Take your teenager to the store with you, or do a chore together. Volunteer to help with one of his chores just so you can spend that time together. Tell your son what you think about your favorite team's loss in last week's game. Ask your daughter what she thinks of the new principal at school. Tell your teenager something you're interested in or discouraged about, and see what happens.

A friend of mine takes his daughter to practice every morning. He told me, "Mandy doesn't talk to us much around the house, and she doesn't say much as I'm taking her to practice—until we are about halfway there. Then, for some strange reason, she decides to have wonderful conversations with me! She tells me what she thinks about all sorts of things. And she asks me for my opinion (believe it or not). That last half of our early morning drive to practice is our best communication time."

It's not so important that teenagers talk at the times we adults deem normal, as long as they talk sometime, somewhere, and in some way that lets them communicate their hearts.

I met with a group of parents recently and asked them two questions. The first one was: "What are your greatest hopes for your teenagers?" I could see the mental wheels turning, but no one immediately responded.

After a few seconds, somebody felt uncomfortable with the silence and blurted out, "That she'll grow up and leave home!" A lot of people laughed. I waited for other responses.

A few more moments passed, and a lady said, "I hope my son marries a good, Christian girl and has a happy family." People nodded. Several other people responded that they hoped their teenagers would mature, have happy marriages and families, and live productive lives. Not very exciting answers.

Then I asked the second question: "What are your greatest fears for your teenagers?" An audible groan could be heard throughout the room. Obviously this was a subject with which they were much more familiar!

Again the answers started slowly. But this time, it wasn't because they couldn't think of what to say. This time they weren't sure they wanted to be so vulnerable in front of each other. The momentum built, however, and soon people took courage from others' honesty. Their responses reflected many hours of thoughts, fears, and prayer requests.

"I'm afraid of losing my little girl," one lady said sadly.

"I fear being a failure as a parent . . . not being able to give my sons what they need," a man related.

"I don't want to explode any more," a lady had the courage to say. "My mom used to yell at me and I hated it, but I'm doing the same thing to my daughter."

Others picked up on this fear. "Yeah, I don't want to do to my children what my parents did to me."

"I'm afraid my children will leave home and never come back," a lady cried softly. "I don't want to be old and alone."

Several comments centered on the difficulties caused by divorce. "I'm afraid they will love their dad more than me," a woman said with a blend of anger and sadness. "And he's never done *anything* for them!"

"The divorce is affecting them more than I thought it would," a man said. "I feel guilty about it too."

"I have such conflicting emotions," an insightful woman stated. "I want to protect them. I want to let them be responsible. I want to keep them as loving little children, but I want them to grow up to be adults too. This confuses me—and I'm sure I confuse them!"

"I guess I'm afraid my daughter will make The Big Mistake—you know, get pregnant, do drugs, get caught stealing, or something like that. What would people in the church say about our family then? I don't like the fact that I worry about what others think, but I sure do!"

Many parents think they do a pretty good job of parenting—until their children become teenagers! Then they realize they've just been promoted from arithmetic to differential calculus, and they missed all the classes in between. Teenagers act very differently than younger children. Often, parents aren't sure how to handle the new struggles and changes. Their best attempts often lead to failure, frustration, and heartache.

So they get angry. They get angry at their teenagers for acting so weirdly, and they get angry at themselves for not responding better to them. Then they feel ashamed for losing control. They may see occasional successes, but there are too many failures. And all of these ups and downs make the parents just as moody as their teenagers.

One reason many parents struggle with their teenagers is that they never sufficiently resolved the very issues their teens face: insecurity, identity, failure, rejection, peer pressure, responsibilities, and intimacy. When parents react inappropriately, they must ask themselves, "What's going on with me? Why am I responding like this?" Many parents are easily threatened themselves, and when their children seem out of control, they react with anger, hopelessness, manipulation, or some other negative emotion to try to cope with the threat. The children want more freedom, but the parents want more control.

Psychologist Lee Carter observed this phenomenon in his book *Family Cycles*.

> The desire to force control in our relationships almost always results in failure. In a predictable way, as we try to exert control over others, the intensity of the relationship grows. Continual effort to control relationships only heightens tension in those relationships. Our well-meaning efforts increase the potential for interpersonal harm. In human relationships, it is true that we have control only over ourselves and no one else. As a part of God's design, each of us was made with the capacity to make choices.[1]

Parents need to be honest with themselves and with God about their feelings and responses to their children. Trying to "suck it up" only creates more pressure and leads to more hurt, anger, and poor responses. They can learn new skills in parenting, but the first step in learning new skills is to be objective about the ones they currently possess—or lack.

Many times, our parenting style is shaped by the model we saw in our own parents. We need to ask, "Am I responding like my father or mother did?" This simple exercise can give us a world of insight into our present relationships with our kids. If we have been hurt by our parents, we need to grieve those hurts. As we grieve, we can also genuinely forgive them. Then, as the hooks of the past are gradually cast off, we can be free to learn new ways of relating. Many parents need new models. Perhaps a parenting class or a small group could help give new insights, skills, encouragement, and accountability for applying these new ways of relating.

As children grow through adolescence to adulthood, we need to gradually treat them more like adults. Responsibility is slowly shifted to the growing teenager so that he or she learns to make good decisions, anticipate and accept consequences, and internalize values. The parent-child relationship gradually changes, and they learn to relate to each other as adults. Adult-adult relationships are based on mutual respect, honesty, and warmth.

Parents need to be honest with themselves about the same threats their kids face: ridicule, insecurity, failure, and the unknown. As parents are more honest with themselves, they can then be honest with their growing, maturing children. Deep and meaningful relationships can then be based on understanding, forgiveness, and honesty.

Recently I received this letter from a parent. It expresses the discouragement of problems in family communication, the hope that it can change, and the determination to do whatever it takes.

Dear Rodney,

I have two teenagers, and for a long time, I thought we were going to have a war. My daughter, Amanda, is up one day and down the next (or the next minute). My son, Byron, only thinks of sports and girls. He doesn't want to help around the house at all. It's like pulling teeth.

My husband, Kevin, has always had the answer for problems in the home: If you yell loud enough and enforce a stiff enough penalty, they'll respond. That worked OK when Amanda and Byron were little, but it isn't working now. Only my husband hasn't changed his plan. He keeps getting louder and louder and making the discipline more severe. And the kids get so angry. Amanda does what her dad tells her to do, but you can tell it just about kills her. Byron has perfected his way of saying "Yes" to his dad and then doing whatever he wants to do.

And I feel helpless. I know there must be a better way, but I don't

*know what it is. I've tried to get Amanda and Byron to talk.
Amanda says everything is fine. She doesn't want to make
waves. And Byron explodes at me about his dad. He makes me
feel like it's my fault that his dad yells at him and doesn't listen
to his explanations.*

*Somehow, I don't think it's Amanda and Byron who need to
change their behavior. It's Kevin and me. It would be a lot easier
if Kevin would change, but I haven't seen any evidence that he is
willing. He won't even talk to me about our need to change at all.
He says he's not the one who is disobedient. They are.*

*But I know I can change—even if Kevin won't. Instead of melting
into the furniture when the yelling begins, I can take a more active role in resolving the problems. Maybe I can offer solutions,
too. And maybe I can develop better communication with the
children so we can prevent some of the problems in the first
place. The grip of anger on our family can be broken, but not by
more screaming and more anger. If Kevin won't change, I will.*

Helen

Listening is part art form and part science. Parents can learn
basic skills, but they also need to apply these skills with understanding and flexibility. As they do, the teenagers' lives will be
richer. And the parents' lives will too.

Some parents have the courage to ask their children for advice
to help them sharpen their parenting skills. You might ask two
questions: *What do you like about the way I treat you?* and *What do
you wish I'd do differently?* I recommend you ask your kids these
simple questions, then let them answer without interrupting,
defending, or correcting.

Ann Landers asked teenagers for advice for parents. Here are
some of their responses.

1. *Keep cool.* Don't fly off the handle. Keep the lid on when
   things go wrong. Kids need to see how much better things
   turn out when people keep their tempers under control.
2. *Don't get strung out from too much booze or too many pills.*
   When we see our parents reaching for those crutches, we
   get the idea that nobody goes out there alone and it's

perfectly OK to reach for a bottle or a capsule when things get heavy. Children are great imitators.

3. *Bug us a little.* Be strict. Show us who's boss. We need to know we've got some strong supporters under us. When you cave in, we get scared.

4. *Don't blow your class.* Stay on that pedestal. Don't try to dress, dance or talk like your kids. You embarrass us and you look ridiculous.

5. *Light a candle.* Show us the way. Tell us God is not dead, or sleeping, or on vacation. We need to believe in something bigger and stronger than ourselves.

6. *Scare the hell out of us.* If you catch us lying, stealing or being cruel, get tough. Let us know WHY what we did was wrong. Impress on us the importance of not repeating such behavior.

7. *When we need punishment, dish it out.* But let us know you still love us, even though we have let you down. It will make us think twice before we make that same move again.

8. *Call our bluff.* Make it clear you mean what you say. Don't compromise. And don't be intimidated by our threats to drop out of school or leave home. Stand up to us and we'll respect you. Kids don't want everything they ask for.

9. *Be honest.* Tell us the truth no matter what. And be straight-arrow about everything. We can take it. Luke-warm answers make us uneasy. We can smell uncertainty a mile away.

10. *Praise us when we deserve it.* Give us a few compliments once in a while and we will be able to accept criticism a lot easier. The bottom line is that we want you to tell it like it is.[2]

You may want to give this list to your child and use it as a basis for discussion. Be sure to listen well.

Reflection/Discussion Questions

1. Did you feel that your parents listened to you? Explain.

2. Think of several conversations you have had with your teen-ager over the past week. Write statements he or she made which reflect values, feelings, or desires. Then write reflecting statements next to these which you can use next time. (You can begin with, "This is what I hear you saying . . .")

3. Write five clarifying questions you can ask to draw people out, gain additional information, and show you care.

4. Evaluate your past listening performance in each of these areas, and describe specific steps you can take to improve in each area.
   - Be observant
   - Be available
   - Be kind
   - Be demonstrative
   - Be wise
   - Be an example
   - Be courageous

5. How can guessing at what your teenager thinks and feels be destructive? What are some alternatives to guessing?

6. What are some positive, constructive ways to respond when your teenager doesn't want to communicate?

7. Do any of these personal issues cloud your ability to communicate? If so, explain.
   - insecurity
   - identity
   - failure
   - rejection
   - peer pressure
   - responsibilities
   - intimacy

8. Which points from Ann Landers' column do you need to apply in your relationship with your teenager? Explain.

CHAPTER 13

The Best Investment You Can Make

In his book *Who's Listening*, Jerry Johnston revealed a study by the Zero Population Growth Institute found it takes $150,000 to raise a child from infancy to the age of eighteen today.[1] But money isn't the only investment in the lives of our children. We need the wisdom of Solomon, the patience of Job, the strength of Samson, the protection of a thousand guardian angels, and more love than most humans naturally possess to invest in our children.

I am convinced most parents don't realize the tremendous stresses their children feel. Even seemingly positive changes like a parent's career promotion and moving to another community can shake a teenager's sense of security. This teenager found herself taking tremendous risks at a vulnerable time in her life.

Dear Rodney,
When we moved to Tennessee, I was a freshman in high school. I didn't know anybody in Nashville. My Dad was transferred in his business. He had been a deacon in our church back in Virginia, and now people expected him to be a deacon in our new church. As soon as we joined the church, I found out that most of the deacon's kids were drinking and experimenting with drugs. There

wasn't really anybody who was trying to walk with the Lord. So as soon as we moved to town, I became a part of the wild crowd. I was very naive, and I didn't know what I was getting in to. They seemed to accept me, and they influenced me. I had always thought of myself as a leader, but I was following them now and doing things I never would have done before.

My dad was so busy in his new job that he didn't know what was going on with me. That contributed to my problem: I didn't feel close to him. I've heard a lot about the absent father syndrome, and I think that was true in my case. I didn't feel accepted at home. My needs weren't fulfilled there. We had been pretty close before we moved, but his new job took him away from me. I was going through a lot of changes at that time. I wanted to dress wild, but he made snide comments about the way I looked. He didn't approve of me at all. There was a wall between us. I thought that anytime I was going to be around him, he would criticize me, so I stayed away from him.

Our conversations became arguments. He'd say, "Where's the old Joyce?" And I'd say, "I'm not the same person I was before we moved." I blamed it on him that he made us move so he could get his promotion.

My mother isn't a very warm person. Instead of talking to me, she'd sneak around and try to find notes from my friends. She "investigated" me. My privacy was violated. She was afraid for me, and she tried to get clues about me. She found out that my best friend was getting into drugs. I wasn't into them then, but I was being influenced. Later, my friend had to be checked into a place to be treated for cocaine addiction. I didn't become an addict because, strange as it may sound, I was so selfish that I didn't want to take a chance on doing something that would hurt me. In our school, girls offered it to me in the bathroom, but I didn't use it. I tried marijuana and I drank a lot, but I never even tried coke or acid. A boy who sat next to me in class told me that if I would sell a couple of sheets of acid for him, he'd give me some free. I said, "No! I'm not going to do that! I'm not going to be your drug prostitute." A couple of weeks later, he got busted. I had plenty of chances, and I made plenty of wrong choices, but

God protected me from doing something totally stupid. Some of my friends got busted. Some got hurt really bad in car accidents from driving when they were drunk. I drove drunk a few times, too, but I never got hurt.

When I was a junior in high school, my best friend was on cocaine and she ran away. My boyfriend broke up with me, and that hurt a lot. He had a new girlfriend, and when I saw them together, that was really hard. My mother was upset with me because I had been caught drinking. She told me that I was destroying the family and my dad's reputation. We had a verbal brawl, and we told each other that we hated each other. It was pretty tense. At that time I had some minor surgery, and I had some pills the doctor gave me. I was at the low point of my life. I had lost my best friend and my boyfriend. My mother hated me. I didn't think either of my parents loved me or approved of me, so I took most of the pills. I don't know if I was trying to kill myself or if I just wanted attention. I started feeling real weird. I told my sister, and she told my mother. She rushed me to the emergency room where they gave me this stuff that made me throw up.

About a week later, my parents put me into a Rapha Treatment Center. I got some really good help there, and my parents got counseling, too. Being there helped me realize the direction of my life and the bad choices and friends I had. That was the turning point for me.

I went with some friends to a football game. We went into the bathroom, and they took these little bottles (like you see on the airlines) out of their purses. They said, "You ought to try one of these." I thought, "Well, I've never tried it before so I don't really know if I want it or not." I knew it was wrong, but I drank it anyway. I didn't like it! It made me feel weird, but I didn't get drunk or anything. But that was the point that other people knew I had started drinking. I can't believe our parents didn't know we were doing this.

A couple of weeks later, some boys offered me a marijuana joint. They were being nice to me, giving me attention, and I liked that. I didn't know what the joint was, but they explained that it would only make me feel mellow. I tried it, and they were right. It did make me feel mellow. I felt really guilty about trying it, and I was afraid I was going to get caught. These boys had heard I had taken a drink in the bathroom at the football game, and they thought I would be an easy target, I guess. Then, almost every day I smoked a joint with these boys.

My first period science teacher told our class that marijuana can cause memory loss and things like that, and that really scared me. The boys had told me that it was harmless, but now I was really scared to use it again. I didn't want to end up as a vegetable. I stopped smoking, but I kept drinking with my friends. That same year when I was a freshman, I went to the lake with my best friend, and I told my mom that my friend's mother was going. My mom, though, called my friend's house and found out that the friend's mother wasn't with us. We had driven down there with some older guys in the back of a pick up with several cases of beer. We had all kinds of stuff. All of us got drunk on the way to the lake. We went to a bar and the bartender fixed me some screwdrivers. I got so sick!

When I got home, my mom told me she had found out that my friend's mother didn't go, but I was so sick I didn't care at all. I threw up everywhere, on my bed, on myself, everywhere. She knew I had been drinking. My mom and dad tried to ground me, but I still saw my friend. I went over to my friend's house and her mother would stay out all night and leave us by ourselves. That wasn't a good situation for us.

My parents kind of gave up on me. I think they were embarrassed. I wanted them to accept me and love me, but I didn't think that was possible because I couldn't live up to their expectations as the "perfect kid," the deacon's kid. My mom was bitter toward me. I couldn't make her happy. She was sick of me. I was too much trouble for her. My dad gave up on me, too. I felt so cold toward them. Sometimes I would wake up in the morning just hating them. I don't know why it was there, but it was.

I wish they would have at least tried to sit down and talk with me. My dad tried to do that, but my mom didn't. She more accused me of things. She didn't ask me to talk to her and explain my feelings and thoughts. She was just mad at me. It would have meant so much if she had wanted to talk to me.

My dad would try to talk to me, but sometimes that just made it worse. He'd say things like, "How can I get up and teach Sunday school on Sunday morning when I can't control my own daughter, and I can't relate to her?" I felt like he was blaming me for being a hindrance to his life and his ministry in the church. I was labelled as the "black sheep." Whatever happened, they pointed their fingers at me. They thought, "If anything goes wrong, it's her fault!" They would even call me a "black sheep" in front of other people. They'd laugh, but they meant it. And once you get that label, you might as well act like it and live up to their expectations. I was mad at the world. I didn't care. I knew they weren't going to accept me anyway, so I might as well hang out with my friends and do whatever I wanted to.

We moved to Mobile after that and I made some really good friends. That next summer, I went to youth camp, and the speaker said that letting God take control of your life is the only way to survive in this world. That's when I became a Christian. From that point, I've really tried to live for the Lord. He's really blessed me a lot.

When I got home from camp, I told them I was sorry for taking so many years off their lives. I had caused them so much grief. I asked them to forgive me, and they asked me to forgive them for how they treated me. It was a wonderful beginning of healing in our relationship.

God has given me a ministry to girls and women who struggle with drugs. Recently I went to an unwed mothers' home. Many of them had problems with drugs, and I was able to lead several of them to Christ. One of them said, "I wouldn't expect you to have the same kind of problems we have, but you can really relate to us." Pressures, temptations, and bad choices can ruin lives even in seemingly strong families.

I don't believe all this was God's perfect will for my life. I made bad choices, but God can turn these around to let me serve Him and help others.

Thanks, Rodney, for understanding.

Joyce

A man once told a group of Christian friends about his trouble with his teenage daughter. Someone said, "We'll pray for your daughter." "No," the man said, "please pray that my daughter's father would reflect God's wisdom and love."

The best investment we can make is in our own relationships with God. As we experience His goodness, wisdom, and strength, we will learn how to express those same traits for our kids too. Just as God always listens without condemning, we can too. Just as He knows when to bail us out and when to let us learn from struggling, we can learn to be wise in responding to our kids too. Just as He forgives us and welcomes us back with a glad heart and open arms, we can treat our families that way too. That investment will pay tremendous dividends in our relationships with our kids.

Speaker and author Jerry Johnston has observed that academic or business success sometimes comes at the expense of the family. Children may be proud of a father or mother's accomplishments and notoriety, but what they really want is time and attention.

Thomas Edison was one of the greatest inventors of all time. He had 1093 patents, including the light bulb, the phonograph, and the motion picture projector. Stories of his devotion to his work were legendary. He worked around the clock with only short naps to rest him for the next burst of creative energy. His son was awed by his famous and driven father. He told his dad, "I don't believe I will ever be able to talk to you the way I would like to, because you are so far my superior in every way that when I am in your presence, I am perfectly helpless." Three days after Edison died in 1935, Thomas, Jr. committed suicide.[2]

Another genius of the early part of this century was Albert Einstein, who won the Nobel Prize in physics in 1921 for his theory of relativity. Einstein's son, Hans Alber, spoke sadly of his relationship with his father, "Probably the only project he ever gave up on was me. He tried to give me advice, but he soon discovered that I was too stubborn and that he was just wasting his time." Einstein's other son, Edward, suffered a mental and emotional collapse in 1929, was later diagnosed as schizophrenic, and was institutionalized.[3]

On a more positive note, some children observe the destructive behavior of their parents and make choices to be different.

Bill Murray, the son of the most outspoken atheist of our day, Madalyn Murray O'Hair, is a strong Christian who speaks powerfully and clearly of his opposition to his mother's teaching. Al Capone was the most notorious of the gangsters of the 1920s. His son, Albert, changed his name to Albert Francis, moved to Florida, and lived a life of honor and integrity. He said, "I want nothing to do with the Capone name."[4]

Studies have shown, however, that like produces like in the vast majority of cases. That is, children tend to grow up to follow the pattern of their parents. Children from dishonorable families who become honorable and upright citizens are few.

Do these stories of famous people with broken family relationships scare you like they scare me? I travel all over the country and meet many people who have made it in every field of business, academics, engineering, medicine, and the church. They have prestige, power, and approval. But I also know the sons and daughters of many of these successful people. Many of these kids would gladly give their parents' wealth and fame for some warmth, affection, and laughs. These kids often feel confused and guilty because they are proud of their parents' accomplishments, but they resent being neglected. These kids also feel guilty for being angry at their parents when other people are in awe of them.

Cliches may be old and familiar, but they remain in our culture's consciousness because they have the ring of truth: *When a person is on his death bed, he won't care how much money he made or what positions of power he held. He will wish he had valued relationships more.* No matter where you are in defining or reaching your life's goals, determine setting relationships as your primary goal. People say you can determine your real goals by looking at your checkbook and your schedule. How you spend your money and your time reflects what your goals *really* are, no matter what you *say* they are. I encourage you to think about your actual goals as reflected in your checkbook and schedule. Do you need to make any changes? If you do, have the courage to make them soon and to stick with them. Value the people in your life, especially your spouse and your children.

As a parent, you can play a vital role in helping to meet needs in the life of your son or your daughter. How do you do that? In Matthew 22:37, Jesus states the Great Commandment: "You shall love the LORD your God with all your heart, with all your soul, and with all your mind."

Let me ask a difficult question. As a parent, have you lived up to this particular commandment? Can you honestly say you love the Lord your God with all your heart, with all your soul, and with all your strength? I will be the first to admit that I've failed to live up to that commandment. In other words, I have failed to make Jesus Lord over every single area of my life many, many times. As Christians, it is crucial that we allow Jesus to give us His wisdom, His strength, and His love so that our motives and behavior honor Him. If He is first in our lives, every behavior, relationship, and priority will be positively affected. What I mean is this: If Jesus is not Lord in your personal life, you can't expect Him to be Lord in your marriage. If Jesus is not Lord in your marriage, you can't expect Him to be Lord in your home. If Jesus is not Lord in your home, don't expect Jesus to be Lord in your children's lives.

Your children are looking for the reflection of Jesus in your life. Most young people today don't see a lot of Jesus in their homes because Jesus is not Lord of the home. This passage of Scripture can be applied to four different areas of our teenagers' lives. Some of these areas may seem quite obvious, but in many teenagers' lives, the needs are hidden and unspoken.

Physical Needs

First, I want to address teenagers' *physical needs*. Many young people rarely receive loving, affirming touch from their parents. They may experience touching from a boyfriend or girlfriend, but this usually has sexual overtones. Teenagers, especially the withdrawn and defiant ones, need the physical affirmation of their parents.

As I read Scripture about the ministry of Jesus, I notice that in many situations, He touched people. He touched the blind, and they were able to see. He touched the lame, and they were able to walk. A sick lady reached out to touch the hem of the garment of Jesus, and He met her need. Psychologists tell us that the human touch conveys security and confidence. Most young people lack security and confidence because they don't feel loved.

They feel like they are unworthy to be loved because they feel they have been failures.

Studies reveal a significant decline in physical and verbal affection from parents as children enter adolescence. For instance, 68 percent of mothers give hugs, kisses, and pats to fifth graders, but only 44 percent physically pamper their ninth graders. Fifty percent of fathers show physical affection to fifth graders, as opposed to 26 percent to ninth graders.[5] We can assume that these dismal statistics fall even further for older teens, so that they receive very little physical affection from their parents at all. It is ironic—and tragic—that kids grappling with their identity and in desperate need of affection receive less at the very time they need more.

Some of us express love very easily; some of us have difficulty. If hugging comes easily for you, keep it up. But if you find it difficult, please try this: The next time your son or daughter walks into the room, go over and give him a big hug. Your teenager may faint trying to figure out what's gotten into you! That's okay. Kids are resilient and he will probably live through the shock. And hopefully, it will become a wonderful habit of expressing love—a habit that communicates the powerful message, "I love you a lot. You are secure and safe with me." And that message can change lives!

Social Needs

Teenagers also have *social needs*. This includes social needs within the family as well as without. Sadly, the average parent spends little time in meaningful conversation with his or her children. Even in Christian families, a recent study reports, the majority of teenagers spend less than thirty minutes a day with their fathers. This includes time spent riding to school, eating meals, watching television, and any other activity which puts teens and fathers in close proximity.[6]

The American Academy of Pediatrics has found that young people spend less than five minutes a day in meaningful conversation with adults.[7] What message does this send? That our kids aren't important enough to take priority over other things. And if we are too busy to spend time together as a family, to whom do our young people turn for advice and encouragement? Their friends. These friends, however, are going through the same problems your son or daughter is going through, and they don't have answers any more than your child has. They are pooling their ignorance!

People are busier than ever before, and relationships are even more superficial. Kids are involved in more things than ever before—activities at school and church—and family life suffers. When I was growing up, I always longed to have a relationship with my dad. We had a fairly good relationship, but because he was always gone, I didn't really have a close, intimate relationship with him like I really longed to have. I would hear my buddies talk about weekends spent hunting and fishing with their dads. I didn't get to do these things very often because my dad was always gone on the weekends.

My dad, however, tried to be there when I needed him the most. I was very athletic in junior high and high school and I can vividly remember playing basketball in a big high school game. Mom sat in the bleachers all by herself during the first half of the game. But as we came back into for the second half, my dad was walking up those bleachers to sit beside my mom. He was dead tired because he had flown halfway across the country to get there in time to see the game. But he made it—just for me. Sometimes he would even close the final night of a crusade and charter a plane just to get home to see me play basketball or tennis. You will never know what that meant to me—that my dad would fly across the country to say, "Rodney, I'm behind you a hundred percent, and I'm here to support you all the way."

If you have a daughter at home, consider taking her on a date once a month. My wife, Michelle, is the oldest of four girls in her family. Michelle's dad used to take each one of the girls out separately once a month. He would ask them questions about their lives, listen carefully, and develop a deeper understanding of their wants, hopes, and needs. He learned what things meant the most to them and how he could demonstrate love to them.

Most young ladies tell me, "I want to have a close relationship with my father, but he doesn't seem to have the time." Men, take your daughters out and get to know them better. Find out what means the most to them. Find out what guy they've got their eye on. Find out what things they are attracted to. Get to know your daughters.

Emotional Needs

Virtually all aspects of a person's life affect his *emotional needs*. Time spent together, special gestures of affection and affirmation, eye contact, listening, and a thousand other things communicate you care. In his insightful books *How to Really Love Your Child* and *How to Really Love Your Teenager*, Ross Campbell says that children (like all of us) have "emotional tanks" which need to be filled up with time, attention, and affection. When they are grumpy, rude, or belligerent, we can be sure that their emotional tanks have been drained by the stresses of the day.

The problem is compounded for teenagers, however, because they often won't talk about their problems. Their drive for independence makes them uncommunicative. The wise parent doesn't press for information at this point. Communicate your support and love, and wait for an appropriate time to gently ask a question such as, "Can I help with anything?" or make a statement which invites open communication: "It looks like you've had a hard day." Don't demand that your teenager tell you everything. Respect her privacy. Your gentle and strong support will be greatly appreciated, even if she doesn't say anything.

Unconditional love is the basis for emotional health. Teenagers need to know that, no matter what they say or do, no matter how badly they mess up, Mom and Dad love them. When young people sense genuine acceptance from their parents, they feel secure. They know they are valued, and their worth is not based on their performance. They are loved for who they are, not what they do.

This doesn't mean that parents should be blind to their teenagers' performance, but they need to focus on what they do well, not what they do poorly. Parents need to become what speaker and author Mamie McCullough calls "good finders," people who look for and point out the good in others.[8] Some parents approach the task of parenting by focusing entirely on correcting and disciplining. Instead, parents need to first look for behavior to praise, compliment, and encourage. An environment of affirmation paves the way formoreproductivediscipline because mistakes and misbehavior can then be corrected in a positive climate.

Spiritual Needs

Last, you can help meet the primary need in their lives, and that is the *spiritual need* to give their lives to Jesus Christ. According to studies by the Home Mission Board of the Southern Baptist Convention, there are over thirty million teenagers in the United States, and twenty million of these do not profess any faith in Jesus Christ.[9] Stories in newspapers and television news programs tell a sad tale of the downward spiral of the youth culture. Hopelessness and despair are the hallmarks of this generation of kids. But Christ and His church can still make a tremendous difference.

As I talk to parents, I often hear parents say, "Rodney, my kid goes to a Christian school. We are very actively involved in our church, and we have a wonderful youth pastor and a wonderful pastor. Our staff is just great, and our church has so many wonderful things to offer. Our youth pastor does so many wonderful things for our young people. He takes them on ski retreats. They are involved in this activity and that activity. He takes them to all these different places." Basically, these parents are telling me that it is the responsibility of the youth pastor and our church to meet the spiritual needs of their children.

Certainly, the church and the youth program can be an important part of your family's spiritual life, but the home is the primary source of spiritual nourishment and direction. Please don't depend upon a youth program to meet all of the spiritual needs of your children! It can't be done. The question remains, "Is Jesus Lord in your life? Is He Lord in your home? Is He Lord in your marriage?" If He is Lord in your home, in your marriage, and your relationship with others, your teenagers will see Him in you. Don't depend upon the youth pastor or church pastor to lead your kids to Christ. You can have the joy of leading them yourselves.

You can also teach your son or daughter how to spend time alone with God. My wife, Michelle, was raised in a Christian home. Actually, she's a preacher's daughter. Her father is the pastor of a large church in Oklahoma City, and he had a tremendous impact on her life. When she was a little girl and got up early in the morning to go to school, she saw her daddy in the living room with an open Bible, having his devotional time with the Lord. She knew that Jesus was first in her daddy's life. He also took the time to teach *her* how to how to have a daily quiet time with God. Her father's example has made a lifelong impact on Michelle, who is committed to spending quality time with God every day. As her husband, I'm grateful to my father-in-law for making a spiritual investment in Michelle's life.

This high school student wrote me about her desire for her parents to help her get to know God better.

Dear Rodney,
It's not that they don't want me to have a quiet time, it's just that they've never personally said "you need to do this—it'll help you grow in your relationship with God." I would consider both of my parents fairly strong Christians—but as far as I know, they don't have quiet times either. It seems like every time I try to start having one regularly, I get interrupted by them coming in. When they do this, most of the time they just act like I'm sitting there doing nothing; they say what they came in for, and then leave. This isn't a big problem or anything, it's just a personal desire I have for their encouragement in this aspect of my Christian walk.
Janice

My parents made a profound investment in the lives of my three brothers and me by teaching us God's Word. They challenged us to memorize Scripture because God's Word "shall not return to Me void" (Isa. 55:11) It is "living and powerful, and sharper than any two-edged sword" (Heb. 4:12). I genuinely appreciate my parents' emphasis on teaching us God's timeless truths. Our lives and ministries are testimonies to God's grace and our parents' commitment.

Sometimes kids are more tuned in to Christ than their parents. In hundreds of conversations with teenagers, I've heard expressed a heartfelt desire for parents to believe in the Lord.

Dear Rodney,

I love my parents with all my heart. They have always cared for me, showed their love, upheld good morals, and been fair. They work hard at what they do and always support me as long as I also try. It might sound like they are the perfect parents and in many ways they are, but their lives are missing the most important thing . . . Jesus Christ.

They both believe in "a" god but think that as long as they live a good life, they will go to heaven. They are very hard headed in this area and won't accept what I say.

My best friend invited me to church for a few youth activities. The first day I went to the church (not youth activities) I was saved. That night, I quit cussing, listening to hard rock, and hanging out with people who do such things. I have made a commitment to wait until marriage for sex and am a virgin. Jesus is a very important part of my life and I badly want to share him with my parents but I can't.

It's not that they won't listen. They just don't understand. When I told my mom I was a Christian, she asked me if I knew what I was doing. When I explained that I let Jesus in my heart, she replied, "Oh," and walked away. How badly I wanted a hug like I had received in church. I got the same response when I went back to church the next week.

When I learn something new about God, I want to be able to tell her about it and I can't. It really hurts sometimes and even worse, I know that if I don't reach her, she will suffer in Hell. I care about them but can't seem to get through. When I have a problem, I can't talk to them. Sometimes when I need them most, they just don't understand.

I have been called to be a youth pastor. I haven't even told my parents about this humungous part of my life because they won't understand. They won't believe in being "called" into the ministry.

This and other things are a big part of my life but instead of the support I want and need from my parents, I get nothing. It hurts that I can't talk to them about my Christian feelings and kills

Susanna Wesley was a busy woman. Wesley lived in the early eighteenth century, before fast food, instant banking, and drive-through windows. And she had nineteen children. She had every reason to be too busy to spend time with her children, but she made her family's spiritual life a priority. Somehow, she carved out time every day to spend with each child.

The fruit of her love later became evident in the work of two sons who hungered for God. John Wesley led one of the greatest spiritual awakenings in history and founded the Methodist Church. Charles's gift in music, combined with his devotion to God, made him one of the most prolific and accomplished hymn writers in the history of the church. Their mother's love for her God and her children—and her commitment to make them a priority in her incredibly demanding schedule—made a difference in the history of the kingdom of God.

Even a gentle nudge from a parent can make a lot of difference. I spoke in a church several months ago, and when I finished my message, I invited people to respond to God's movement in their lives. During my talk, I had noticed a young woman sitting in the back with an older lady, probably her mother. Sometimes, you can just sense that God is working in a particular person's heart, and I felt that way about this young woman. But when I gave the invitation, she didn't respond. I prayed under my breath, "Lord, please work in her heart!" But she stayed on the back row.

At the very end of the service, I felt the Lord telling me to encourage people to respond. I said, "If you are standing by a friend or family member who doesn't have the courage to come forward, put your hand in their hand and invite them to come to Christ." I watched as the mother put her hand in her daughter's. They said a few words to each other, and suddenly, the bonds of fear in that young woman's life seemed to break. The two of them stepped into the aisle and walked to the front of the church.

As they came closer to me, the young woman looked up and our eyes met. Immediately, she put her hands over her face and began to weep. I walked to her. She kept her face buried in her hands as she sobbed, "Please, I don't want you to see me. I've been so bad—there's no way God can forgive me."

I tried to comfort her by taking her hand, but she pulled it away from me. I said gently, "I want you to look at me for just a moment."

"No!" she said through her tears. "No, please don't look at me! I've done some really bad things. God can't forgive me."

I said to her, "Do you believe Jesus died for you?"

She paused a second, and said with a sigh, "Yes. Yes, I do."

"Do you also believe that God can change people's lives? Maybe even yours?"

"I don't know," she said honestly. "I'm willing to let Him if He will. I'll try anything." Suddenly, she took one hand from her face and reached out to grab my hand.

I said, "Would you be willing to pray to the Lord with me?"

"Yes," she said haltingly. I prayed for a moment, then she asked Jesus to step out of heaven and into her life.

I've heard more eloquent prayers, but none more beautiful. The very moment she said, "Amen," she looked up at me with tears streaming down her face. But these weren't tears of sorrow. They were tears of forgiveness and hope. She smiled and told me, "Rodney, I feel so different! For the first time in my life I feel as though a ton of bricks has been taken off my shoulders. I've carried the load of shame and guilt for so long! But tonight, for the first time, I feel free!"

Later she would tell me her story of sexual promiscuity which stripped her of dignity and threatened to ruin everything good in her life. But at this moment, she was basking in the forgiving and cleansing grace of Jesus. Before my very eyes, I saw a passage of Scripture come to life. Paul wrote to Titus:

For the grace of God that brings salvation has appeared to all men, teaching us that, denying ungodliness and worldly lusts, we should live soberly, righteously, and godly in the present age, looking for the blessed hope and glorious appearing of our great God and Savior Jesus Christ who gave Himself for us, that He might redeem us from every lawless deed and purify for Himself His own special people, zealous for good works. (Titus 2:11-14)

The grace of God produced big changes in this young woman's life!

When parents observe and help meet their children's needs, kids feel safe and loved. When parents model a life of love, strength, and hope, kids follow that example. The demands on our time and energies are enormous, but so is our responsibility to be good examples to our families. Millions of kids don't have good models. They grow up in broken homes or in homes where bitterness or apathy take the place of love and care.

Many of us are familiar with a lovely poem written by Dorothy Law Nolte, called "Children Live What They Learn." We would do well to use it as a benchmark for our relationships with our children.

Children Live What They Learn

If a child lives with criticism,
He learns to condemn.
If a child lives with hostility,
He learns violence.
If a child lives with ridicule,
He learns to be shy.
If a child lives with shame,
He learns to feel guilty.
If a child lives with encouragement,
He learns confidence.
If a child lives with praise,
He learns to appreciate.
If a child lives with fairness,
He learns justice.
If a child lives with security,
He learns faith.
If a child lives with approval,
He learns to like himself.
If a child lives with acceptance and friendship,
He learns to love the world.[10]

Reflection/Discussion Questions

1. If an objective person evaluated your checkbook and your schedule, how would he describe your values? Explain.
2. How can you help meet your teenager's:
   - physical needs
   - social needs
   - emotional needs
   - spiritual needs
3. What changes will you make in order to meet these needs?
4. What resources do you need in order to make these changes?
5. Reread the poem, "Children Learn What They Live." Which statement stands out to you? Explain.

CHAPTER 14

When Tough Love Is Appropriate

One of the most difficult tasks a parent has is knowing when to back off and let a young person succeed or fail on his own and when to strongly and boldly confront behavior that is out of control. This mother realized she was too involved in her daughter's life. She was smothering her child and preventing her from making decisions. Her choice was to back off.

Dear Rodney,
When my daughter, Darbra, was out of control, I felt out of control, too. I tried everything I could think of, but the frustrating thing was, none of them worked. I tried to reason with her to convince her what was the right way to act, but she didn't listen. Sometimes I went off to my bedroom and cried. I felt so helpless that I was powerless to change her or help her. Sometimes I escaped by reading endlessly. And sometimes, I hate to admit, I resorted to hand-to-hand wrestling with her. We were both so angry and nothing else seemed to work, so I guess our frustrations just came out in physically trying to make the other person do what we wanted.
After many years of this, I realized that I couldn't control Dar-

bra no matter how hard I tried. I think this is the whole point. I had to let go and trust God to work in her life.

Instead of trying to manipulate her behavior, I tried to overlook much of the negative things and say positive things about her ability to learn to handle situations for herself. I encouraged her to pray about these things, and I told her I was praying God would give her wisdom. I had to grit my teeth when she experienced the consequences of her bad decisions.

I was afraid Darbra would make the wrong decisions without me. I hoped she would need me and ask for my counsel, but too often, I tried to force these on her. I knew she was not ready to face the adult world. And I was right, but there was nothing I could do to make her make better decisions.

It's hard letting her be an adult.

Janie

We want to treat adolescents as adults so that they learn communication skills and responsibility. Sometimes, though, they refuse to respond as adults. When rebellion, addiction, or defiance fosters patterns of irresponsibility, the most loving thing a parent can do is set limits and enforce consequences. These are painful choices. They are usually made after other means have failed, as this mother relates.

Dear Rodney,

My children were basically raised in a single parent home, though their father and I are married. He is in the Army and has been stationed overseas for long periods of time. From a very young age, I taught my kids to be self-reliant and to make their own decisions based on what I had taught them. I make them independent thinkers, but when they started making their own decisions and expressing their opinions, I was not sure I was happy with their choices—because they weren't my choices. I had to learn to back off, listen, counsel, and not intervene directly. Most of all, I had to learn to let go and not say: "I told you so" when their decisions were bad ones. I had to be supportive, understanding, and encouraging so they would continue to trust me with their mistakes as well as their successes.

All this worked pretty well with Bryan, my oldest. But I'm afraid I'm losing with Karen. I've tried so hard to let her make her own decisions, but she's ruining her life. And mine, too. A year ago, I found out from another mother she was smoking marijuana. I confronted her about it and tried to reason with her. She got very angry at me, but she quit. I thought that was the end of it. But a few months later, the school called to ask me where she was. I told them she should be at school. When she came home that night, I asked her how things went at school that day. She said, "Oh, the usual." I hit the roof!

The school told me she had several unexcused absences. I pleaded with her to tell me what was going on in her life, but she insisted it was "no big deal" and for me not to "get so bent out of shape about such a little thing." That response didn't calm my fears! I also found out she was spending a lot of time with some boys who had a reputation for having only one thing on their minds.

The past several months I've felt angry and hopeless. I've pleaded. I've screamed. I've grounded her so often that she basically stays grounded, but it doesn't seem to work. I don't know what to do to help her turn her life around. There are so many horror stories of my friends' children who have destroyed their lives by making bad decisions. I don't want that to happen to Karen. But I'm afraid it already has.

Rodney, I hope you can help kids like Karen. And I hope you can help me, too.

Faith

Some parents make the mistake of using anger to control their children. They assume that yelling, cursing, throwing things, scowling, or nagging will be a sufficient deterrent to misbehavior. And it usually is for a short while. But the law of diminishing returns comes into play, and it takes increasingly higher levels of anger to control the children. As a result of this process, both the parents and the teenagers lose respect for each other.

Other parents use the opposite tactic. They can't stand the conflict, so they retreat. They talk about everything in the world except the real issues that need to be addressed. They overlook even the most obvious red flags because they simply cannot bring themselves to face the facts. One mother said she had no idea her son was sleeping with his girlfriend. When her son heard this, he laughed. "I've been taking my girl to my room in our house for months. Sometimes we walked right past my mom!"

Denying, excusing, and minimizing are easier (in the short run) than the conflict of addressing the problem. The mother of an anorexic girl may say, "Oh, she's not really that thin. I think she wants to be a model." A father hears that his son is arrested for vandalism and shrugs, "Boys will be boys!" A mother feels guilty for working outside the home, so she ignores the neighbors' concerns that her son is beating up kids in the neighborhood. She doesn't want to communicate that he has a problem because somebody may blame her. A dad doesn't say anything to his fourteen-year-old daughter who is dating an eighteen-year-old because he's afraid she'll tell him she's sleeping with her boyfriend.

Our children need clear expectations with clear consequences. As they grow and mature, they may have a role in determining their rules and consequences, and therefore will probably be more committed to them. The simplest way to establish expectations and consequences is to write them out. Include rewards for good performance, such as an increased allowance, and consequences for poor performance, such as a reduced allowance. The expectations can cover everything from chores to grades to communication with siblings. "You don't have to *like* your sister," one mother told her son, "but you have to *be kind* to her."

Consequences should reflect the things each child values. For instance, a boy who enjoys watching television can be rewarded with a certain amount of TV time if he does well in his expectations. Conversely, TV time is lost for poor performance. Make sure you clearly establish your expectations and consequenses before implementing them. You may need to negotiate to be sure each person thinks the system is fair. Remember, your goal is not only performance; you also want to foster responsibility and communication. Expectations and consequences will change as the child grows and as interests and needs change. Anticipate these changes so you will not be caught off guard.

Clearly stated expectations and consequences allow you to

remain calm when you have to enforce them. "This is what you agreed to," you might say. "I'm sorry you didn't make it. I hope you'll do better next time." Use your judgment on being flexible in enforcing the consequences. If a teenager has been very conscientious in almost every area and has been under a lot of deadlines at school, you may choose to give grace on some chores around the house that didn't get finished. If you are flexible, be sure to communicate the positive reasons of your willingness to flex—that will be encouraging—but let the son or daughter know this is an exception. Don't make a habit of giving in, or the plan won't work at all.

Sometimes clearly defined boundaries are enough to help your teenager avoid destructive habits and cultivate a relatively stable and problem-free life. Sometimes they are not. Occasionally (and unfortunately) the stress of adolescence creates a crisis for teenagers. Look for danger signals in your kids if you suspect they are having inordinate problems. You don't need to probe too deeply. There are signals which are quite evident to the objective observer. Look for:

- changes in the circle of friends, music, or clothes
- frequent or unexplained absences from home
- changes in eating or sleeping habits
- problems at school or at work (performance or relational problems)
- explosions of anger or withdrawal and depression
- patterns of deception and unusual secretiveness
- inordinate mood swings
- lack of motivation and self-discipline
- unexplained possession of large amounts of money, or the need for large amounts of money
- using excuses to cover irresponsibility
- increased health problems
- poor personal hygiene
- glazed expressions, dilated pupils
- unwillingness to communicate
- loss of interest in previously enjoyed activities and friendships
- concealed firearms, knives, explosives, or other weapons

A parent's first step in facing a teenager's destructive pattern of behavior is usually to plead for them to change. That doesn't work, so the parent threatens. That doesn't work either, so he or she pleads harder and threatens more. The only result is that the parent gets more and more frustrated.

People don't change unless they are desperate. Protecting your teenager from the consequences of his behavior keeps him from becoming desperate, and the destructive pattern is allowed to continue. Yes, the teenager needs to change, but perhaps the parents need to change as well. If you cannot force your child to cease his unacceptable behavior, you may have to take a different approach.

At some point, you may need to consider an intervention as a tool to stop the self-destruction of your teenager's life. Interventions should be led only by experienced counselors or pastors who can walk the family through the process of preparation, communication, and follow-through. Ask your pastor, counselor, or school counselor to help you find that competent, experienced person to serve as the facilitator. The steps most intervention facilitators include are:

1. The parents and the facilitator need to determine the exact goal of the intervention. In many cases, the goal will be to obtain treatment for an addiction to drugs, food, or something else. The consequences for lack of cooperation should be clearly identified and agreed upon.

2. The facilitator meets with a select group of people who hold authority over the teenager. This can include parents, a coach, teacher, youth pastor, and possibly a relative or two from the extended family. Siblings can be included if they are mature. In this meeting, the facilitator communicates the clear goals of the intervention and the steps taken to implement it. Each person is asked to prepare a three-minute, objective, factual presentation for the teenager, describing how his or her behavior is destructive and harmful.

3. Participants are asked to be prepared for the person's possible and probable reactions to the confrontation: an-

ger, tears, self-pity, transferal of blame, sudden agreement (to get the meeting finished in a hurry), or genuine repentance. Also, the participants are asked to be prepared for their own reactions: fear, anger, blame, guilt, or a sudden desire to "rescue" the teen.

4. The teenager is invited to a participating person's house without knowing what is planned. All of the participants are already there. When he walks in, the facilitator takes charge, asks him to sit down, and says something like, "We love you, and we want the best for you. That's why we're here tonight. I want to ask you to be quiet and listen to us. After we are finished, you can say anything you want to say." The facilitator then asks each participant to give his three-minute presentation. Afterward, the goal and the consequences are presented so the teenager can make his choice.

5. If the teenager takes the intended step, the process of healing begins. This is a long process with many ups and downs! He may decide to quit at any point. If so, the consequences need to be reiterated and enforced.

6. The participants may also need some attention after the intervention. The facilitator may choose to call each person or meet with them after the intervention to answer any questions and help each person process the experience.

Interventions are intended to confront the teenager's problems, but they can also reveal parents' problems. All individual problems are, in fact, family problems. All family members are affected by each person's problems. Everybody needs answers, comfort, and healing.

If you have questions about treatment options for members of your family, I want to encourage you to call Rapha Treatment Centers. I have had a long and very helpful relationship with this organization. They provide Christ-centered care for people who struggle with all kinds of emotional problems, and they provide this care for both adolescents and adults. To find out more about Rapha Treatment Centers, call 1-800-383-HOPE.

You can't make somebody in your family healthy and happy, but you can play a vital role in providing hope and resources to meet deep needs. Tough love is a painful path for parents, but sometimes, confronting destructive behavior is the most positive and loving thing we can do for our kids. This path is never easy. It reveals latent emotional distress in us and in others in the family. But if we have the courage to press on, God can use it to radically change lives. Even ours.

I received this letter from a brave mother.

Dear Rodney,

I know my son, Bobby, was having problems, but so was I. My husband, Lee, lost his job after his heart attack a couple of years ago. The combination of the medicine, the heart attack, the hard time he had getting a job, and the financial crunch at home all combined to make life miserable for Lee. He felt like such a failure. He became deeply depressed. He tried several jobs, but he didn't do very well in any of them. He was an assistant manager of a hardware store, but he'd never worked in hardware before. All the details were over his head. And then he got a job as a traveling salesman. He enjoyed people, and getting out of the house was good for him in some ways. But he was gone overnight a lot, and he started to drink again. I guess he felt so lonely in hotel rooms.

My son was fourteen when his dad had the heart attack. He had always done so well in school, but for some reason, he started failing classes he had been making A's in. I guess we didn't give him the attention he needed. Some people say that is a very important time in a boy's life. But we did all we could. Lee was depressed and trying to get back on his feet. I was working to earn some money for the family. Our daughter, Melynda, was coping OK with it all. (She's three years younger than Bobby.)

By the time Bobby was sixteen, he was pretty wild. All the boys he hung around with were children of good friends of mine, so I thought it was OK. I didn't ask too many questions—maybe because I didn't want to know the answers. There were some signs, but I didn't see them. He came home really late. He didn't talk to us about much. He got really angry rather quickly. His grades fell off to C's and D's. He got calls from a lot of girls who I thought were kind of loose.

But like I said, I was preoccupied with taking care of my husband, making some money so we could pay off the doctors and have enough to eat, and take care of Melynda. I just didn't have enough energy to cope with anything else. The pressure was so intense, we got on each other's nerves a lot. Everybody was mad about something—or a lot of things. We used to laugh and talk in our house, but during all this, you could cut the anger in the air with a knife. All of us were miserable around each other.

I couldn't believe Bobby would drink. Surely he could see what whiskey was doing to his father! But he was drinking a lot, and smoking cigarettes and marijuana. It was incomprehensible to me that he was doing all this.

After he graduated from high school, he wanted to go to college with his friends, but we didn't have enough money, and his grades weren't good enough for a scholarship. He went to junior college here in town while his friends went to state universities. He was miserable at home. When he went to visit them, I had visions of them dating nice girls and going to nice parties after the football games. I found out later that they had, well, drunken orgies all weekend.

Lee got so mad, he often yelled at Bobby, and the yelling got louder and more frequent over the months. But that just drove Bobby away. He drank more, and who knows what else he did more of. The madder Bobby got, the sweeter Melynda got. I'm glad for my sake, but there was a big strain in the two children's relationship. They hardly spoke to each other any more. And Lee's drinking got worse, too.

I'd just about come to the end. I couldn't take it anymore. I laid awake and cried night after night, but I didn't want anybody to hear me. Liz is a friend of mine whose husband is an alcoholic. She put up with it as long as she could, then, years ago, she called another friend to see what could be done to help her husband. They got several people together and talked to him and told him he had to stop or he would lose his job and everything else he had. It was a struggle for him, but he stopped drinking. His life really changed.

But I didn't know how to do that with two people at once. I didn't know who needed it more, Lee or Bobby. I told Lee that I wanted to have Liz and her husband over to see us to help us confront Bobby about his drinking, sex, and money problems. But Lee wouldn't have any part of it. He said Bobby was doing OK. That's a pretty strange thing to say about somebody you scream at and call a failure almost every day. So we didn't do anything. I felt so helpless and alone. I wanted to do something, but I didn't know how.

This went on for seven more years. During that time, Bobby got married, his wife had a baby, they divorced, and Bobby got married again. He had lost four good jobs which I had helped him get. He spent all his money on drinking and partying. His life was a wreck, but you could always see him laughing and drinking with his buddies, so he didn't look like a wreck. Finally, I decided to do it on my own if Lee wouldn't cooperate. I told him what I was going to do, and I guess I scared him. I thought he would put up a fight like he did before, but he didn't.

Liz and her husband came over and helped us work up a plan. We called Bobby's current employer, and she told us she was going to fire Bobby if he didn't straighten up soon, so she said she would help us confront him. We worked out a time for the five of us to see Bobby. He came over, thinking he was going to have dinner with us. He came in and sat down in the den, and I called to the other room to have the others come in. All of us were really nervous, especially my husband. I wasn't sure he could make it through it all.

I started and told Bobby why we were there. He got really mad, and he got up to leave. Liz's husband jumped in and explained how people who loved him had talked to him the same way years ago, and he told Bobby how glad he was that he hadn't walked out then. Bobby sat back down. Each of us told Bobby we loved him and we wanted him to be happy. My husband didn't say much. Liz's husband told Bobby he needed to get a grip on his life, and stop ruining his health, relationships, and career. He asked Bobby to go to a chemical dependency support group at our church, and he told him he would be glad to be Bobby's sponsor.

I wish I could say that it all went smoothly after that, but it didn't. In fact, it got harder. Bobby went to the meetings, and Liz's husband actually became like a father to Bobby. That's where part of the problem was. As Bobby changed, I saw some things in my life that needed to change, too, but Lee refused to even talk with us about these things. And Lee deeply resented the relationship Liz's husband had with Bobby. It seemed that all of us were on the same page except Lee.

A few weeks ago, Liz saw I was really down about Lee. She knew Bobby was doing a lot better, but there are new strains in our family. She asked me if I would do it over again, and I told her, "Yes, I would. I can't help it if Lee refuses to get help. I'm not willing to sacrifice Bobby—or Melynda or me—because Lee won't admit he needs help." I hoped Lee would see his own needs as we all went through the changes with Bobby, but he didn't. Yes, I'd do it again. It's been hard, but it's been worth it.

Suzanne

I asked some good friends of mine to share their stories with you. Kelly is a young woman whose adolescent years were traumatic. I think you'll find her words gripping, and in the end, inspiring.

Rodney,
When I went into junior high, I was really nervous. I started to gain a lot of weight. I didn't feel pretty. I didn't have a lot of boyfriends like some of the other girls. I gained weight so I could get some attention. I know that doesn't make sense, but that's what I thought would help.

Then when I was a freshman in high school, I met a boy named Will who was the first person who looked beyond my weight and totally accepted me for who I was. I felt a lot of pressure because I wasn't pretty. My sister is beautiful, but I'm not, so when Will came along, his acceptance meant the world to me. He was two years older than me.

My dad didn't like him even from the very beginning. I didn't know why he didn't even give him a chance. Maybe if dad had been more accepting, maybe I could have seen the truth about Will. Instead, it took me a long time and a lot of heartache to see what Will was really like. Dad said, "I don't want you to spend time with Will. I've heard some really bad things about him." My dad didn't give him a chance, and being the kind of person I am, I wanted to be the person to give Will the chance he needed. I thought he was a good person down deep inside, and I thought I could be the one to bring it out in him.

Will was really big, and since he was even bigger than me, I felt pretty around him. He wasn't very attractive, but he made me feel pretty. He made me laugh and he made me feel good about myself. He encouraged me to be my own person and to think for myself. That sounded great, but later, I realized that he was pulling me away from my parents so I would do what he wanted me to do. I had never been close to any boy physically before. It felt really good to be close. I felt wanted. But the more physical we got, the worse our communication got. Instead of talking, we got more involved physically.

The deeper my relationship with Will progressed, the worse my relationship with my parents became. They didn't want me to date him. They didn't allow me to be in a car with him. I wasn't allowed to be alone with him anywhere. We weren't allowed to even go to lunch at school together. I think all these strict rules—"Don't do this. Don't do that. There are people watching you. Don't think we won't find out."—that kind of stuff just made me really angry and want to get around the rules. I didn't care what my parents said!

My mom and I didn't have a very good relationship because we are so much alike. She saw what was going on, but she didn't know how to communicate with me. She got really frustrated and stopped trying to talk to me. She just sent me to my dad. That really hurt because it felt like she didn't even care. My dad was really angry at me. At one point they sent me to a counselor in our city. We came to an agreement that I would go to counseling and they would be more lenient with Will.

My dad didn't even let me present my case. He didn't listen or give Will a chance. He already had his mind made up about Will. My mom just cut me off because she didn't know how to deal with it. Both of them were really angry, and I withdrew from them. I wanted to see them as little as possible. We stopped communicating almost completely. I knew I was hurting them, but I felt so trapped. I didn't see any way out.

Sometime in there, Will became emotionally and even physically abusive. I was really scared, and I told my counselor about it. She told me he had big problems, and that if I really cared about him, I needed to let him work out his problems apart from me. So I decided to give him some time and space because I wanted what was best for him. When I told my parents I was going to back off from Will, they were totally excited! We had a little reunion in our home because they felt they had the family back together again.

The problem was that Will wouldn't leave me alone. My parents took me out of school and had a teacher come to our house to tutor me. They tried to isolate me totally from him, but somehow, he got messages through to me. At first, I didn't want it. He kept crying and saying things like, "I can't live without you!" or "If you really care about me, don't abandon me!" He really played with my heart. I tried to talk to my parents about getting back together with him, but they said, "No. You need to stick with your commitment."

The pressure built up so much that Will and I ran away together. My parents wouldn't let me go anywhere by myself, but finally, I convinced them to let me go to church with a friend. I told my friend that I had to go to the bathroom, so I walked out of the youth group by myself. Will picked me up at the bottom of the stairs. I had already packed my bags and put them over the fence at home. One of his friends picked us up and took us to the bus station. We took the bus from Ohio to Tampa.

I'll never forget that bus ride. We took a lot of old clothes and tried to disguise ourselves so no one would recognize us. We were afraid the police would be after us. We called back to Will's friend, and he told us that the police had put out an APB on us and were questioning a lot of people. While we were on the bus, I was so scared. It kept going through my mind, "What are you doing? What are you doing? Is this the kind of life you want to have?" I knew it wasn't right, but I felt so trapped! I didn't see any way out.

When we got to Tampa, Will's mother picked us up. We went to her house. She said my parents and the police had called her to try to find us, but she lied to them. She told them that she didn't know anything about us. I remember being really frightened. It was the worst time in my entire life. Things were really good between Will and me because he felt he had defeated my dad. But I was miserable.

After a couple of days, I called my parents. My sisters were bawling, and I was bawling. On the phone, all I heard from my dad was his anger. He didn't seem hurt at all. And I was furious at him for that. I felt really sorry about my mom and my sisters because they were bawling, and I knew I had hurt them so much. Will and I flew back to Ohio. I moved in with my counselor. We worked out a deal that I could see Will, and I would go to counseling with my parents. The first time we saw each other in the counseling office, I hugged my mom and dad for a long time. I felt some happiness with them for the first time in a long, long time. All I ever wanted from my parents was acceptance . . . no matter what I had done. I felt so bad because I knew I had messed up, and I was afraid they would never love me again . . . like there was no turning back for me. They told me things like, "We live in a glass house. Don't you care how our family looks?" But I kept saying, "But don't you care about me? You think what other people think of us is more important than how I feel!" My parents wanted us to be the perfect family, above and better than anyone else. But I didn't want to be perfect. I just wanted to be accepted . . . even with my mistakes and being overweight and everything. My dad was big in physical fitness, and my sister is a beauty queen. I always felt inferior . . . unwanted.

My relationship with my mom and dad is wonderful now. They've forgiven me and I feel total acceptance from every person in my family. I love to come home from college and just be with them. The change started soon after Will and I came back from Tampa. My parents and I were seeing the counselor, and she told them, "You need to accept her and love her and not be so strict with her." We were working on our relationship, and I tried to work on my relationship with Will, too. When I tried to pull back from him, he said he would kill himself.

One night, my parents and I met with a youth pastor who listened to my story. He was brutally honest with me. He said, "You need to break up with this guy, and you need to do it tonight." His confidence gave me confidence. I called Will, and that night, I told him our relationship was over. It was hard. I had a lot of conflicting emotions, but I knew it was right. Will blew up! He threatened to kill himself again, but he didn't. A few months later, he and his family moved away.

A few weeks after I broke up with Will, my family went on a little vacation together. In that hotel room, the beginning of total healing took place. I felt free again to be the person I wanted to be. My parents were so loving and forgiving. I moved back home, and our relationship changed and grew day by day. My mom and I are exactly alike. That's why she couldn't communicate with me. Now I understand what she was going through. She felt it was all her fault because she hadn't raised me right, and she felt really guilty. She wanted to be the perfect mom, and now she felt like a complete failure. She was bitter toward me for a long time, but we talked about how we had hurt each other and forgave each other. Now my mom, my dad, and my sisters (this is not an exaggeration) are my best friends in the whole world! I go to them before I go to anybody else.

The Lord has let me experience all this to help me grow and so I can help other girls. Now I can talk to friends who are going through difficult relationships. If I can help just one person, it's worth it.

Kelly

Reflection/Discussion Questions

1.   What are some reasons parents don't want to be painfully honest with their teenagers? Which of these, if any, are true of you?

2.   Write a paragraph explaining your response to this statement: Sometimes the most loving thing we can do for someone is to impose consequences on their behavior.

3.   Examine the danger signals in this chapter. Have you seen any of these in your teenager? Explain. When is looking for danger signals a counterproductive witch hunt?

4.   Read the steps involved in an intervention. Have you ever participated in an intervention? If so, explain the purpose and the outcome. What would you do differently next time? Who can serve as a facilitator if you ever need one?

CHAPTER 15

In Conclusion . . . Meeting Your Child's Unspoken Needs

As his birthday approached, a freshman in high school was asked by his mother, "What do you want?"

His response was quick and sure. "A Ferrari. A red one, please. A new soccer shirt, a mountain bike, four tickets to the concert next month, and a trip to the beach with my friends."

His mom smiled and said, "I was thinking more about a new rubber ducky for your bath!" They both laughed.

Adolescents have a lot of dreams and wants. They can usually list a host of things they'd like to have, but when they genuinely reflect on what's important to them, they have far more insight than many parents might expect. They don't need all the trappings of rich, cool kids. They don't need for you to drive a newer car or have a bigger house. They want your attention and affection. Even though they seem to scream, "Leave me alone!" they want attention. When they fail, they know it. You don't need to point it out. And when they succeed, don't make too big a deal out of it. It's only a test or a game. They'd rather you get excited about them—but not too excited, and in private, of course!

Teenagers need:

Stability

In their world of constant change, they need to know that they have a solid center for their lives, a point of reference to always come back to. Many things can change, but they need to know they can always count on you to consistently care for them, love them, see their good points, and comfort them when they hurt. To many teenagers, consistency is the hallmark of stability.

Dear Rodney,
All I need from my parents is their unconditional love which I do get most of the time. I need them to treat me equally in considering my brother and sister. I also need them to understand my feelings and thoughts.
For starters, I need them to treat me equally and not treat my brother and sister more generously. For example, I might do something wrong and get grounded for a month or two. But if my brother or sister do the same thing they just get a lecture. Another example of this is when I have a piano recital or a band concert on the same day as my sister or brother who has a concert or something. They will end up going to my brother's or sister's engagement.
I also need to be trusted with my own decisions. For example, If I hear a new compact disc on the radio, which just happens to be my favorite group in the world then she start asking me all these questions about it like, "Is it rap? Is it music? Is it something I would like; and how bad do you want it?" I would answer these questions and still not get the compact disc.
What I need from my parents might not be what's best for me. But if something is good for me I really need it.
Denise

Attention

Sure, they're pulling away, but they need enough time with you for you to pick up on their signals. Some teenagers talk openly and freely with their parents, but most force their parents to become mind readers. Notice changes in eating and sleeping habits, their circle of friends, and choices of music and clothes. Also, be observant about the circumstances that seem to trigger particularly good or bad moods. You don't have to be James Bond to see most of the signals, so don't try to read what isn't there. Just be observant and ask a question or two, especially about the good things in your teenager's life.

Some adolescents are far down the path of sexual experimentation or drug use before their parents ever even ask one question. The signals were clear, but the parents were too preoccupied or afraid to hear the truth. The truth may be frightening, but it is better to deal with reality early than when the teen is far down the road.

Fairness

Every person needs expectations, but we also need to be a part of setting those standards in our lives. Involve your kids in the process. Ask them what time they should be in on weekends, how much they should be allowed to drive the car, how much they should pay for the insurance, how much and what kind of television shows to watch, what chores they should do around the house, what grades are acceptable, and any other expectations and privileges that are age appropriate. And get their input, too, on the consequences for noncompliance.

Many parents have a merit system for their teenagers. For instance, if your daughter gets a 3.0 this semester, keeps her room and bathroom reasonably clean, and is home on time when she goes out, she may get to use the car one more night a week next semester.

The teenagers' penchant for justice makes them rebel at any rules which are imposed in a harsh or arbitrary way. Keep the communication lines open, and involve your adolescent in the decision-making process. Make the consequences consistent with the offense.

Forgiveness

All of us make mistakes, but adolescents make more than their share because they try so many new things. They want more freedom, they resist authority, and they are moody. Parents need to observe the example of the father in the story of the prodigal son and graciously forgive. Though Christians talk about forgiveness often, many of us don't really know much about it. Forgiveness is not holding a debt or an offense against a person (Matt.

18); it is refusing to take revenge for the offense (Rom. 12). True forgiveness requires two elements: First, we need to be honest about the offense, not excuse it, minimize it, or deny it. And second, we need to experience Christ's forgiveness ourselves so we can forgive others out of our own rich experience. The apostle Paul wrote: "And be kind to one another, tenderhearted, forgiving one another, even as God in Christ forgave you" (Eph. 4:32).

A girl in junior high wrote me about her experience of forgiveness.

Dear Rodney,

A couple of months ago, my parents got in a big argument. I know what I did was absolutely wrong and I regret it every single passing day. I guess that it was one of those spur of the moment things and I'll just have to live with it unfortunately. This is how it all began.

I was at a school basketball game. Some of my friends and I were all laughing and giggling about a joke we heard when Rachel suggested we walk down the road about five minutes to McDonald's. I decided that it was perfectly fine except one thing. My parents told me before I left not to go. No exceptions. Of course my friends had already made up their minds, and I certainly wasn't going to change them, so I went along with them. We ate our Big Macs and our fries and we were on our way back to the game when the red beast pulled up unexpectedly. It was him, my father. I crawled in the passenger seat. He gave me that terrifying look. That horrible, mad, get away from me look.

I ended up getting grounded from the phone and I missed a party. The atmosphere the next couple of days in our house was foggy. I was a coward. At dinner the next night my mother said something that upset me. I snapped and blurted out, "It's no wonder my sister ran away! It's because of you!" Then I ran to my room and cried for what seemed like hours. As I lay there thinking about everything, I felt so horrible. I tried to get myself to apologize the next day but I just couldn't bring myself to do it. My mom wasn't on speaking terms with me and I was treated like dirt. I was about to leave for school in the middle of making a sandwich for lunch when my mom walked in. I told her that I apologized and I told her everything I had been feeling the last couple of days and she understood. I had hurt her deeply but she still loved me. Now my mom and I are the closest of friends. I'm very thankful for that. Every day I try to judge my actions. I won't pull a dumb stunt like that again. You can count on that.

Eve

Forgiveness is a unilateral act. The other person may not be sorry, may not repent, may not even admit he did anything wrong. But we still can forgive. If we don't, our hurt turns to resentment, and our resentment turns to bitterness, and bitterness strains every motivation and relationship in our lives.

But forgiveness doesn't mean we don't hold people accountable. And it doesn't mean we have to trust the person. A friend's teenage son sneaked out of the house late one night and drove his buddies around town until four o'clock in the morning. His father caught him, and said to him, "Son, what you did was wrong. I want you to know that I forgive you, and I love you enough to be sure you experience the consequences for your actions. You won't be allowed to use the car for three weeks. After that, if this happens again, it will be a long time before you can use it again. Do you understand?" His tone was calm but direct. He then hugged his son to reinforce his love for him.

One of the reasons some of us don't forgive is that hatred gives us energy, and the thought of sweet revenge makes us feel alive. Some of us hold onto our bitterness because we are afraid of the changes and responsibilities which come with forgiving others, but bitterness exacts a price in us.

Frederick Buechner wrote:

Of the Seven Deadly Sins, anger is possibly the most fun. To lick your wounds, to smack your lips over grievances long past, to roll over your tongue the prospect of bitter confrontations still to come, to savor to the last toothsome morsel both the pain you are given and the pain you are giving back—in many ways it is a feast fit for a king. The chief drawback is that what you are wolfing down is yourself. The skeleton at the feast is you.[1]

Zig Ziglar wrote:

Forgiveness takes the burden of hate, guilt and bitterness off your back and with a lighter load, you can climb higher and faster, and be much happier in the process. . . . Forgiveness is tough, dangerous and exciting. Tough because of our human nature. Dangerous because it forces us to take responsibility for future progress. Exciting because it frees us to become our best self.[2]

All of us appreciate being forgiven. It is the basis for building healthy relationships.

Dear Rodney,
I am due in court today for vandalizing a car. My step-father has never once told me that he loved me or said I really was his son and that he trusted me. But today before the trial he sat me down and said to me, "Son, as long as you tell the truth, I will love you. I trust that you will tell the truth." That made me feel really good. He has never said that to me before. His saying that to me made me realize how much I really love them. My parents may not be Christians, but they are the sweetest two people I have ever met. My mother has her share of problems and my step-father isn't exactly a real saint. But I realize how much I love them.
William

Honesty

And we make mistakes too. When we do, we need to have the courage to be honest about it. That goes a long way to establishing credibility and communication with a justice-minded teenager. It may be difficult, well worth it to say, "Son, I was wrong. Will you forgive me?" After a number of times, it'll get easier.

A teenager wrote me:

Dear Rodney,
I want you to know that my relationship with my Dad used to be really horrible. When I was younger, he had some health problems, he lost his job, and he was really hard to live with. Now I realize that he was depressed, but at the time, all I knew was that he was really angry at everybody and everything. Nothing I did—or anybody else did—was good enough for him.
To tell you the truth, I hated him. I don't like to admit it, but I did. But something happened in the past two years. I don't know

what it is, but my Dad has changed so much. About two years ago, I heard him say something I never ever thought I'd hear from him. He asked me if we could talk. I was afraid because every time he had ever "wanted to talk," he griped at me for something. But this time, he said something like, "Marian, I have treated you badly by being so critical of you. I'm sorry." I just about fainted! We cried and hugged.

And over these past two years, Dad has told me several times that he has been wrong for yelling at me or griping at me. I know it's hard for him to be honest, but it lets me be honest about when I'm wrong, too.

I feel bad about hating my Dad those years when we didn't get along. I think he feels bad about those years, too. But things have changed. Now, we're friends! I never would have imagined that we could have the kind of relationship we have now. My Dad's honesty has been the door to a whole new relationship!

                                                                    Marian

Love

Some kids are easy to love. They are sweet, kind, thoughtful, and affectionate. It is second nature to go over and give these kids a big hug and say, "You're terrific! I sure love you!" But being around many teenagers is like living with skunks and porcupines. Every time you get near them you either get a rotten smell or get stuck.

These kids need our affection just as much as the others—maybe more. It would help us if we understood that they act that offensive because they feel so badly about themselves—unloved and unlovable. They desperately need us to see the good in them (which may take some excavation), overlook much of the offensive behavior (which may take some blinders), and give genuine, heartfelt affection (which may take the grace of God).

It is difficult to get water from a dry well, and it is difficult for parents to express love to their children when they feel so emotionally empty themselves. The answer is not to "just try harder." Parents who have no love to give need to find a support group so they can share their hopes and frustrations, be affirmed, and learn to express love to those who don't seem very loveable.

Teenagers aren't the only ones who struggle for a sense of identity. Often, each person in the family jockeys for attention. This emotional elbowing leaves some hurt and alone, some hurt and defiant, and a few feeling superior. Parents want their families to be safe havens for their kids, but they need to understand the fact that each person is trying to carve out a sense of being special.

Several factors determine how a teenager feels about his or her family. These include the parent-teenager relationship, the sibling relationships, the level of perception about reality, and the teenager's own personality. Let's examine each of these.

Parent-Teenager Relationships

Undoubtedly, the most significant factor in how the teenager feels is his relationship with his parents. To the degree he feels safe, understood, protected, and provided for, he will probably feel grateful. However, his *perception* of reality is more important than *actual* reality for determining his feelings, so if he doesn't feel he is safe, he won't act safe.

Protection and provision may seem easy to accomplish, but often the subtleties go unnoticed by parents. For example, one child may continually and harshly pick on another. If the victimized child's complaints are brushed off with, "Oh, don't make such a big deal about it," the victim will feel unprotected and unloved. Sibling squabbles are a part of every family, but if the parents aren't sufficiently involved in resolving disputes and complaints, feelings can be deeply wounded. And provisions are not only for food and clothing, but also for time, attention, and affection.

Perhaps the most common complaint of teenagers about their parents is: "No matter what I do, it's not good enough." They believe that their parents nag and criticize them to the extreme. We need to be sure to focus on the good in our teenagers' lives and affirm these traits and achievements over and over again. Our affirmation will make them much more willing to hear when we need to instruct or correct them.

Sibling Relationships

These relationships can be one of the greatest sources of strength—or heartache—in a person's life. When they champion each other's causes, comfort each other's hurts, and understand each other's concern, they produce hope and strength. Too often, however, the desire to carve out an identity produces a one-up-manship mentality. Each person has to do better, go farther, and be smarter than the other, and the easiest way to accomplish this goal is to put the other one down. Some rivalry is normal, but parents need to provide an environment for resolution of these seemingly insignificant, yet tremendously important, conflicts.

Perception of Reality

Ironically, teenagers with the most difficult family relationships often say the most positive things about their families. And kids from safe, secure families feel confident enough to express negative feelings about their families. From the outside, an observer could draw very opposite and wrong conclusions.

Abuse victims (and others who feel unsafe for any reason) defend the abuser for a number of reasons. The victim desperately wants to believe the abuser really cares, so she tells herself and others that he does. She wants to avoid the explosions of condemnation that honesty would produce. And she fears the condemnation of others in the family for betraying the family secret.

Pressure to be a "good Christian family" leads to the same behavior of denying the reality of problems in order to protect the facade of perfection. Some spouses and children are told (verbally or nonverbally), "Don't rock the boat! It's important for us to be good examples, so don't let anybody know about our problems!" The identity of a good Christian family takes precedence over honesty and the resolution of problems.

Personality

Some children are sensitive; some are clueless. Some are aggressive; some are comatose. Some are leaders; some follow. The personality of a teenager, especially in connection with the personality of other family members, is a significant determining factor in how he feels about the family. Many different personality profiles and tests are available today. Most of these measure the goal orientation and the relationship orientation of people. The intricate interplay of these traits in the person, and the dynamic of personalities in the family, produce peace or tension.

For example, a strong, dominant child who loves challenges will naturally test the rules of the family. If the mother is strong, too, there will be conflict—continual and intense—with the child. A sensitive, creative, shy child will feel overwhelmed by an energetic, loud, flamboyant father. The dad will wonder what's wrong with his kid. There's nothing wrong at all. The child is simply different, *very different*, from his father.

When family members begin to understand each others' personalities, they often say, "Wow! No wonder we've had problems understanding each other. You and I see things very differently!" And this realization forms the basis for better communication in the future.

Teenagers are growing and changing in many ways. They are making the incredible transition from childhood to adulthood. It may have been okay to treat them like little kids in the past, but not anymore. They want, they expect, they *demand* respect as young adults (even though they sometimes still act like children). How do you spell strong, safe, secure, growing teenagers? R-E-S-P-E-C-T.

If I could take you with me across the country and let you listen to thousands of young people as they pour out their hearts, you would hear several recurring themes. It is too bad that parents often are the last to hear these messages from their children. Teenagers desperately want their parents to meet their needs, but far too often, they will remain unspoken needs. This letter epitomizes the hearts of many thousands of young people:

Dear Rodney,
I really need my mom and dad. Sure, I am almost grown. For all practical purposes, I can take care of myself. I support myself almost totally when it comes to financial matters. Most kids would love the freedom I have. At least they think they would. But they don't understand how lonely that freedom is.
I would give anything if they would just take an active part in my life. I would give anything if they asked me how my day went, or who is the new girl I am dating. But they don't, and their lack of interest hurts me so much I ache inside. I am nineteen—but I still need my parents so much every day. Just because I am older physically does not mean I need their support any less. In fact, I

need them more. I need that support so much. I need to know they love me. I need to know that my life matters.

Other kids who complain about things like having a curfew and bringing their dates home to meet dad don't realize how much they have, how lucky they are. Oh, I wish my parents did. I do need them. I need their guidance, as well as their support in the decisions I make. These same decisions are the ones that are shaping my whole life. Although, I like to think I have made sound decisions so far—their input and active involvement would have made those decisions so much easier.

All I want is for them to love me. I only want them to take an active part in my life. Really, that's not an option for them it is a requirement. But I guess in the hustle and bustle of everyday life my parents forgot about that.

Bill

Reflection/Discussion Questions

1. Have the letters in this book helped you understand your teenager's unspoken needs? If so, explain.
2. Write a specific plan (including who, what, when, where, why, and how) to provide your teenager with:
   - stability
   - attention
   - fairness
   - forgiveness
   - honesty
   - love
3. How can you be involved in developing these:
   - parent-teenager relationship
   - sibling relationships
   - perception of reality
   - personality
4. Reflect on the goals you wrote for questions 1 and 2 at the end of chapter 1. How well have you accomplished these goals?
5. What do you need to do now to continue to accomplish these goals, find needed resources, and strengthen your relationship with your teenager?

A Personal Word from Rodney

Hopefully by now, God has used the stories and information in this book to reveal many unspoken needs in your child's life. However, as a parent, perhaps you have discovered some unspoken needs in your own life. One of the best things you can do is begin making some new commitments to yourself, your spouse, and your children. Remember, it is never too late to start doing what is right.

However, you will never live up to those commitments without God's help. If you would like to invite Christ to be the Lord of your life and begin a new life of forgiveness and hope, I want to invite you to pray this simple prayer.

Dear God, as a person and as a parent, I ask You to forgive me for my many sins. I confess I can't continue to live my life without You any longer. I believe with all my heart that Jesus Christ died on a cross and arose again to give me a new beginning. From this day forward, I put my trust in You to help me become the person and parent You want me to be. Thank You for giving me a new hope to live for. In Jesus's name, Amen.

If you prayed the above prayer or you have a personal story you would like to share with me, please write me. I look forward to hearing from you. Please write to:

Rodney Gage
P.O. Box 820553
Fort Worth, Texas 76182

Your friend in Christ,
Rodney Gage

Notes

Chapter One

1. Josh McDowell and Dick Day, *Why Wait?* (San Bernardino, CA: Here's Life Publishers, 1987), 388.
2. Zig Ziglar, *Raising Positive Kids in a Negative World* (New York, NY: Ballantine Books, 1989), 46.
3. Ibid, 77.
4. Cited in Ziglar, 180.

Chapter Three

1. Archibald Hart, *Adrenaline and Stress* (Dallas, TX: Word), and *Stress in Your Child* (Dallas, TX: Word).

Chapter Four

1. Robert S. McGee and Pat Springle, *Getting Unstuck* (Dallas, TX: Word/Rapha, 1992), 26.
2. These statistics have been compiled from figures published by the Children's Defense Fund and the book *13th Generation* by Neil Howe and Bill Strauss.
3. McDowell and Day, 40.
4. Ziglar, 5.
5. Les Parrott, III, *Helping the Struggling Adolescent* (Grand Rapids, MI: Zondervan, 1993), 97.

Chapter 7

1. These statistics have been excerpted from *National Guidelines for Comprehensive Sexuality and Character Education*, published by Medical Institute for Sexual Health, Dr. Joe McIlhaney, Director, 1994.
2. Susan C. Weller, "A Meta-Analysis of Condom Effectiveness in Reducing Sexually Transmitted HIV," *Social Science and Medicine*, 36:12 (June, 1993).
3. *National Guidelines*, 9.
4. *National Guidelines*, 9-10.
5. Cited in *National Guidelines*, 3.

Chapter 8

1. *USA Today*, 11 April 1994, 1f.

Chapter 12

1. Lee Carter, *Family Cycles* (Colorado Springs, CO: NavPress, 1993), 15.
2. *Dallas Morning News*, 31 December 1988.

Chapter 13

1. Jerry Johnston, *Who's Listening* (Grand Rapids, MI: Zondervan, 1992), 15.
2. Jerry Johnston, *How to Save Your Kids from Ruin: Winning Strategies for Raising Rock-Solid Children* (Wheaton, IL: Victor Books, 1994), 20-21.
3. Ibid, 20-21.
4. Ibid, 20-21.
5. Josh McDowell, *How to Be A Hero to Your Kids* (Dallas, TX: Word, 1991), 22.
6. McDowell and Day, 386.
7. Cited in Rodney Gage, *Let's Talk About AIDS and Sex* (Nashville, TN: Broadman Press, 1992), 46.
8. Ziglar, *Raising Positive Kids in a Negative World*.
9. Dean Finley, *Southern Baptist Youth Statistics*, from a newsletter, 1992.
10. The poem, "Children Learn What They Live," by Dorothy Law Nolte, is often published under "author unknown" and appears to be in the public domain.

Chapter 15

1. Frederick Buechner, *Wishful Thinking: A Theological ABC* (San Francisco: Harper and Row, 1973), 2.
2. Ziglar, 281, 286.

About the Author

Rodney Gage has spoken face-to-face to over two million students in public and private schools across North America. Rodney is nationally recognized as an effective communicator on contemporary youth issues. He has appeared on numerous television and radio talk shows and has been featured in many newspapers and religious magazines. He has conducted over 300 crusades in evangelical churches.

Rodney is a graduate of Liberty University and Southwestern Baptist Theological Seminary. He is the author of *Let's Talk about AIDS and Sex*. He and his family live in Dallas, Texas. They are members of Prestonwood Baptist Church where Dr. Jack Graham is pastor.